treasures in clay jars

treasures in clay jars

new ways to understand your church

X - bk's primary purposes x, xi, 8

mov't → institut 28f

George B. Thompson Jr.

Foreword by James W. Fowler

THE PILGRIM PRESS
CLEVELAND

TO *W. Widick Schroeder, Professor Emeritus*
The Chicago Theological Seminary

for inspiration through

scope of knowledge
meticulous analysis
academic quality
and friendship

The Pilgrim Press, 700 Prospect Avenue East, Cleveland, Ohio 44115-1100
pilgrimpress.com
Copyright © 2003 George B. Thompson Jr.

Scripture quotations, unless otherwise noted, are from the New Revised
Standard Version of the Bible, © 1989 by the Division of Christian
Education of the National Council of Churches of Christ in the United
States of America and are used by permission.

Printed in the United States of America on acid-free paper

08   07   06   05   04   03   5   4   3   2   1

Library of Congress Cataloging-in-Publication Data

Thompson, George B. (George Button), 1951–
    Treasures in clay jars : new ways to understand your church /
George B. Thompson, Jr. ; foreword by James Fowler.
        p.   cm.
    Includes bibliographical references.
    ISBN 0-8298-1566-X (alk. paper)
    1. Christian leadership.   2. Church growth.   I. Title.

BV652.1.T48   2003
253—dc22

                                        2003065610

CONTENTS

FOREWORD

George Thompson has brought all of his experience as a pastor, and his learning as a student and teacher of the social sciences, to the writing of this book. There are many authors who write about the church and church leadership in theological terms. There are many studies that place emphasis on strengthening the church through Christian education or pastoral care. Some vital sources on congregational leadership draw constructively on family systems theories. Others work from the standpoint of organizational and leadership studies.

Thompson brings a vigorous sociological perspective to inform pastors' understandings and practices of ordained and lay leadership in congregations. Written with clarity and the use of many examples, Professor Thompson, almost in a conversational way, shares with the reader the fruits of his study and practice of congregational leadership, and the ways churches can keep their ministries vital in the midst of changing circumstances.

While never forgetting the central importance of pastoral leadership, this book invites lay leaders in congregations to look at the church as a dynamic social organism. Thompson helps the reader understand the social patterns of community and neighborhood life. Using well-known examples from business, he stimulates pastors and churches to stay alert to "what time it is" in the community and the neighborhoods in which they live and worship. Like human beings, churches too have life cycles. Thompson shows us that there are patterns of church beginnings, struggling early years, and the emergence of gradual or rapid momentum. And then, for a variety of reasons, there likely will be the turn to decline. With what I would call "faithful realism," the author provides pastoral and lay leaders with tools that will help them discern the present situation and movement (or "stuckness") of a church and its membership.

Without judgment, and with an encouraging affirmation and the offering of useful tools, Thompson invites pastors and congregations to look lovingly but clearly at the communities of faith that we call our churches. He is convinced that pastoral and lay leaders who are willing to face the real conditions and challenges they face do not need to proceed blindly and without options toward inevitable church decline.

I commend his book to any reader who wants to develop an in-depth understanding of congregations as organizations and as systems. Thompson's stories, examples, and teaching provide a clear set of lenses for taking a fresh look at churches and their challenges. We who live and lead, and who are committed to nurturing and strengthening the churches we know, can benefit richly from the teaching and examples offered in this book. For vestries, church councils, and the other governing or leading bodies of congregations, this book makes a good source for deepening joint understandings of their churches and of the ways they can be helped to flourish.

—James W. Fowler

C. H. Candler Professor of
Theology and Human Development
Emory University

PREFACE

Readers of these pages should prepare to feel somewhat disoriented—but hopefully also a bit exhilarated. I am trusting that this book will bring you the kind of eye-opening insights that eventually led me to write what follows. As you pass through those confusing moments that accompany any authentic learning, I am hoping that your sense of the potential for these resources will grow.

Loren Mead, a student of and advocate for congregations, made the case a number of years ago that things are changing for the Church.[1] Among many others, Mead has argued that we today are witnessing the end of one dominant model of Christianity. The social, political, and economic dynamics that gave rise to the familiar forms and practices of Christian faith for millions (especially in Europe and North America) have shifted. Those dynamics will not "pop back into place" and allow those of us comfortable with the old paradigm to settle back into business as usual. So what is taking its place? Prognosticators can and do make their best guesses, but no one knows for sure.

This book, then, can help all of us to understand what is happening to the old forms of Christian faith in our world today, as well as help us shape the new forms. However, that is not its primary purpose. Instead, it seeks something of a preliminary, cognitive function. As I reflect theologically and biblically upon the enterprise outlined here, I am drawn time and again to Jesus' words to the twelve as he sent them out on a healing mission: "so be wise as serpents and harmless as doves" (Matt. 10:16). This stark contrast of images is framed by yet another contrast, that of "sheep in the midst of wolves." In this text, Jesus minces no words in describing the kind of poor treatment that the twelve can expect in their travels. Almost enigmatically, Jesus' admonition to be both dovelike and serpentlike arrests my imagination. I think Jesus would have had a tiny smile on his face as he presented those seemingly contradictory images.

What makes the most sense to me, in our twenty-first-century context, is to read this text as a call to hold in tension two styles that appear naturally to repel each other. On the one hand, we are drawn by our faith to idealism and seeming innocence—the dove. Especially for those of us with theological training, the dove makes sense. We are eager to follow its idealistic vision. Yet, on the other hand, Jesus also tenders in this text the repulsive image of the serpent, that creature who led our primal ancestors Adam and Eve astray. Surely this wily, disgusting creature offers no redemptive virtues or practices! Yet there it is, out of the mouth of Matthew's Jesus, to the inner circle of those whom he called for special work. What gospel purpose could it possibly serve?

Let me suggest an answer to this troubling question. It is that Jesus wanted his followers to be street smart, to understand "worldly wisdom," so as to utilize it for the benefit of gospel ministry. Jesus was not arguing for capitulating to standards that would deny the gospel its power; remember, the use of the serpent image is in tandem with that of the dove. It is that very tandemness, that need to associate the two, that gives rise to the kind of ministry to which Jesus sent the twelve. By being both wise as serpents and harmless as doves, Jesus' followers could undertake very challenging work with conviction, courage, and effectiveness.

The primary purpose of this book, therefore, is as a tool for constructing creative gospel partnerships between what the Church proclaims and what the world actually is like. Differences between the way things are and the way things ought to be are the grist for ministry—and they need to be understood better. In the Church, our idealism has a long tradition in the disciplines of theology. In today's world, our awareness of how humans actually behave has been advanced significantly through the disciplines of the human sciences. This book introduces some of the resources of those disciplines to the Church, suggesting how they can help church folks approach any ministry "wise as serpents" while living like a dove.

Books like this one are not conceived out of purely intellectual or speculative interests. As I will suggest in chapter 1, my interest in this topic grew out of my experience as a pastor. Graduate courses in sociology and organizational theory fed my effort to understand better what occurs in the parish. In the Ph.D. seminar each spring, I listened to colleagues address various real-life issues by constructively thinking theologically, at the same time using tools from political science, economics, psychology, sociology, and anthropology. In more recent years, I have applied tools like those in these chapters while consulting, coaching, and training pastors and other church folks.

Yet I do not see this book as a full-blown introduction to the social sciences per se. Rather, the focus here is upon stretching our often implicit vantage points and, in doing so, pointing out "new" resources for ministry. Readers who utilize such resources will be engaging a "both/and," rather than an "either/or," methodology. This book represents the broad perspective out of which I teach, write, and assist congregations. My other two books happen to build upon concepts from anthropology. That is, they are more narrowly framed, because of the nature of the particular practical ministry issues addressed in them respectively. Readers interested in helping their congregation discern and follow fresh vision,[2] or pastors seeking an overview of the challenges and opportunities for ministry and leadership[3] might want to look at these other works.

Those readers who are in training for ministry are the primary focus for this present work. Rather than attempt to spell out specific practices based on the ideas, this book encourages readers to reflect upon the difference to one's approach to ministry that these several approaches suggest. Certainly pastors can fit into this category, but the "show-me-what-to-do" pastor will be disappointed here. On the other hand, pastors, associates, religious educators, youth ministers, music directors, outreach coordinators, and other church program staff all can benefit by framing their work in new ways. I hope, then, that this book will be used in Bible colleges, theological and divinity schools, other graduate programs in ministry, continuing education events, certificate programs, church-based leadership development programs, and so forth. Since I am Protestant, my presentation necessarily is shaped by this tradition. Yet it should be fairly easy for readers in Roman Catholic, Jewish, and even Muslim contexts to see how these cognitive tools illuminate their religious environments as well. Certainly, too, bishops and other denominational officials who work with congregations are encouraged to read this book. Sometimes we cannot see a workable solution to congregational issues until we first find a new perspective on it. Denominational officials can be most useful to the churches in their charge by offering such guidance.

Once again, I thank Ruth Hicks and Robby Carroll for reading the manuscript and providing encouragement and insight. In her capacity as Associate for Ministry for the Presbytery of Greater Atlanta, Ruth works with pastors and churches daily. Her wisdom is always helpful and gracious. Robby's experience as a pastoral counselor and marriage and family therapist broadens my appreciation for the context of the church-helping business. Dr. David Forney, Associate Dean of the Faculty of Columbia Theological Seminary, read the manuscript with enthusiasm and a careful eye to detail. My faculty colleagues at the Interdenominational Theological Center provide a hospitality in which my energy for teaching flows easily into the task of writing. Editor Kim Sadler continues to be supportive with friendly gusto, as she affirms my writing interests and offers the kind of guidance that editors must provide.

One final introductory word: Don't read this book unless you genuinely seek to become an effective agent for gospel witness. Many new and sound resources are available to help you with the dovelike side of faith. Here is one that will assist you with the serpentine side of the equation. May it be put to good use. May your gospel work see you slithering through the world skillfully, while maintaining a cooing transparency of purpose.

ONE

HORSELESS CARRIAGE

Why Another "New" Paradigm?

TOOLBOXES AND THE PASTOR

I love tinkering around the house. If there were no doorknobs to tighten, no locks to replace, no rooms to repaint, no lawn to mow, no rooms without ceiling fans—well, you get the picture! Even though the projects often have their frustrating moments, I still get distinct pleasure in maintaining and improving the piece of real estate that I call home.

Besides needing experience, the home tinkerer cannot get very far without the right tools. When I graduated from college, my mother gave me a gray Sears Craftsman toolbox. She wanted me to have at least the basic hand tools, since I was heading out into the real world. As the years went by, I added now and then to the box. Some of the tools, of course, do not fit in the original toolbox and must be stored under the workbench, or hanging on nails in the wall. Certain tools work for a lot of different projects—hammers, screwdrivers, wrenches, measuring tape. Others are specialized—log splitter, miter box, glass cutter. A few of the tools in my modest collection are especially dangerous unless used carefully and correctly—the chain saw, for instance, even though it is electric and has just a sixteen-inch blade.

Even though I am grateful to have each one of these tools, I don't think about them that much. For the most part, tools are not objects of adoration, since their purpose is to help you get something accomplished. There are times during my home projects when I realize that a slightly different tool would make the job go easier. And probably the only way that I come to that conclusion is that I have used the tool that I possess enough to know how to use it effectively. Tools make our lives easier, and knowing how they work gives us a sense of both satisfaction and accomplishment.

During the first decade of my work as a pastor, I had a growing feeling that something seemed to be missing from my minister's toolbox. I had taken seminary courses in the usual fields from which budding pastors prepare for the practice of ministry—preaching, worship, pastoral care, education, administration. In those early pastoral years, I served as an assistant pastor of a medium-sized church in a growing town, as pastor of a small church in a rural area, and as an associate pastor of a large church in a small city. Because each position and church setting was different, I entered each one eager to learn ways to do that ministry effectively. I sought out workshops when the opportunities were available; I read articles and books about church leadership that dealt with various congregational issues. It seemed to me that I was making the most of my seminary training and continuing education.

Yet I still felt that something was missing, casting its shadow out there somewhere, a vague shape that I did not recognize. As my pastoral experience broadened, I began hearing myself saying things like, "This is beginning to look familiar; what is it?" and "I don't remember dealing with this in seminary!"

Consider this early pastoral experience of mine in light of the following stories—one historical and another personal.

THE HORSELESS CARRIAGE

One of the "tools" that has changed all of life more dramatically than few others in history is the one that we commonly refer to as the "automobile." This machine-turned-revolution commenced scarcely a century ago. A series of mechanical inventions were brought together by enterprising folks in various ways: their results eventually created a self-propelled contraption that could carry people faster, in vastly more directions, and more conveniently than even the reigning monarch of transportation, the railroad. Life on the planet today would be unimaginable without this contraption. It increased the mobility of humans and their "things"; it stimulated new forms and practices of social status; it contributes to the loss of thousands of human lives each year; and it raises atmospheric ozone to unhealthy levels. As we know it, the personal "car" is one tool without which our world barely could exist as it is.

Nevertheless, in its early years, this contraption that we now take so easily for granted was considered a novelty, a passing fad. The very first models and units were expensive, were hard to start and steer, moved as slowly as barn animals, and were rendered immobile in the mud. Most people initially thought of a four-wheeled carriage with a loud engine as something quite frivolous. Horses were more reliable and, when one had to travel a distance, the railroad would get you there.

Indeed, the early name of these contraptions that we now call "automobiles" reveals the paradigm that American society used at the time for thinking of personal transportation. This name, as you probably know, was the "horseless carriage." A carriage was like a large crate or box, either enclosed or open, in which persons and cargo could be "carried" (hence, the noun "carriage") over distances. Propulsion for carriages was provided by large animals such as oxen or cattle, but most frequently they were drawn by horses. Carriages carried persons of all classes and walks of life; they were common and necessary at the close of the nineteenth century.

No wonder, then, that the new form for getting around was described in terms of the familiar form. The first "cars" were carriages that did not depend on horses for energy: they were "horse-less." It was not until sometime after Henry Ford began mass-producing his version of these new contraptions that their new name "auto-mobile," ("self-moving") became the common one. This new term, then, signaled a change in the way that people thought about getting around. The transition from horse-drawn carriages to gasoline-powered automobiles was a paradigm shift—one of tremendous proportions.

HORSELESS CARRIAGES AND TOOLBOXES

Once I lived in a house that was ripe for major renovations. The attic space was large, high, empty, and dusty—in that condition, it was pretty useless. Working with that space in such a way so as to create a living area called for careful design, calculated supplies, and tools. For this attic project, most of the hand tools in my steel Craftsman box were far outclassed. Technically, I could have used them to do most of the work, but the results would have been questionable. My hand tools would have taken absurdly too long; each task would be that much harder to undertake; and some of them would have been downright dangerous. Only when I *acquired* tools designed for the tasks at hand was I prepared to tackle the attic. Not only this, but I also had to work with a project specialist, a general contractor. This person had the experience and skill to move the project from design to completion. Some of the tasks I could perform, as long as I was given specific instructions and some oversight. In this manner, the work moved along safely and with the eventual desired outcome. I never once had to say to myself, "If only I had had that tool instead of this one, things would have turned out better."

What does this renovation story have in common with the history of the early automobile? Both of them deal with paradigms, those assumed models of "how things are and are meant to function," models affecting the way that we live, think, and behave. Paradigms, most of the time, are taken for granted. We don't have to think about them, because they do what we expect them to do. However, in those times when paradigms begin to falter, or when new experiences challenge us, what then? How many times do we try to make a familiar paradigm work again before entertaining the possibility that the paradigm itself has run its course? At some point, hand tools don't do the job. At some point, it's not a "horseless carriage" anymore.

As a young pastor, I think that what I often was experiencing about ministry was that the paradigms were faltering. My ministry models were based on my experiences growing up in my home church in the 1950s and '60s and then, in the 1970s, being active with college Christian fellowships before receiving seminary training. The frustrations that I felt in those early pastoral years cannot be attributed only to the level of my personal growth or my naïve professional readiness. As I have said, I felt like something was missing from my pastoral toolbox. I had been prepared for a horseless carriage, but what I encountered were automobiles.

A TOOLBOX DESIGNED FOR THE JOB

Over the years, what slowly and painfully became plainer to me were my own inherited paradigms. My basic seminary training had focused heavily upon human experience in its individual expression. When we students had reflected theologically about human existence, we centered upon the experiences and needs of persons. We took courses on effective pastoral care to individuals, drawing carefully upon the latest thinkers in psychology. We learned theories and techniques to make education more interesting and rewarding to each participant. Preaching class considered how to make the sermon speak meaningfully to the person in the pew. Without any explicit intent, our ministerial preparation reflected the individualism so familiar and accepted in American society.

There is no question that Christian faith speaks to the condition of each human being. Yet treating the individual as though she or he exists primarily in isolation violates our very experience. To be human is to be more than individual; it is also to be in relation—connected, in both subtle and dramatic ways, with other humans. Furthermore, because human beings associate with each other for a vast array of purposes and needs, we must take seriously our experience collectively.

On Its Own Terms

Slowly, then, over the years it occurred to me that congregations themselves are distinguishable phenomena in their own right. This might seem obvious to you, but it came as something of a revelation to me. Social human experience is real, and it constitutes the life of every church. Just as psychologists and psychiatrists observe and name common features and behaviors within individuals, so also students of society note common social patterns. Being one type of human group, churches express patterns of activity that are not entirely idiosyncratic. Congregations are, in many respects, like other groups.

As a young pastor, I was beginning to realize that the several congregations that I had served looked and behaved in many ways very much alike. This was the case in spite of obvious differences that perhaps were not as significant as I had thought at first. A fresh dimension of understanding, a new perspective, had begun to make its case. Its shadows were appearing to me more frequently, enticing my mind in their fleeting but mute witness.

In more recent years, I have been delighted to discover that those persistent shadows that I had been glimpsing were cast largely by the great riches of the social sciences. My seminary friends and I had talked a lot about "the Church" and "community," but the language had been heavily theological, that is, normative—"the way things should be." Once I began to see how collectively based categories and concepts could be applied to the experience of congregations, it was like a fireworks display in my mind. The lights and colors began going off everywhere!

"A Pair of What?"

This fireworks display that I experienced with the social sciences did not come to me quickly or easily. Certainly there were some moments when I felt a little like Martin Luther must have felt with his hermeneutical turn on the Epistle to the Romans. While such moments (for me significant analytical turning points) seemed quite sudden, they actually occurred after years of growing uncertainty. I was going through what Thomas Kuhn claims is necessary when scientific research makes major, new discoveries.

In his classic essay, *The Structure of Scientific Revolutions,* Kuhn argues that scientific disciplines function with "paradigms" that shape interpretation of research data—and even of what research actually seeks. That is, to do any scientific work at all, there first must be an acknowledged framework for the inquiry, one that inevitably "restricts the phenomenological field accessible for investigation."[1] Consequently, to some extent, what researchers expect to find often influences the study significantly.[2] It is not until researchers actually perceive that their received data does not fit the paradigm that they begin to consider that they might need to see the data in a new way.[3] The discovery experience in science therefore is actually a process, Kuhn argues. It involves both seeing something new and eventually creating terminology that presents a new notion for what is observed.[4]

One of the implications of Kuhn's line of argument is that tradition and novelty always end up in the same soup, whether recognized or not. That is, when scientific work is seen as "normal," its conventional laws and methods practically and necessarily dictate. Paradigms of normal science guard, so to speak, the nature of all inquiry at the time; they by nature withstand incongruity in data. It is not until these inconsistencies "penetrate existing knowledge to the core" that changes in the existing paradigm begin to be considered.[5] In other words, the model of research itself provides the mechanism for realizing that a particular result does not fit: "Anomaly appears only against the background provided by the paradigm."[6]

Kuhn's primary argument, then, concerns the question of how novel scientific paradigms materialize. They do so over time, within a field of study, as researchers gradually come to terms with uncertainties and the power of their own discipline's models. Kuhn summarizes this argument with these words:

> Because it demands large-scale paradigm destruction and major shifts in the problems and techniques of normal science, the emergence of new theories is generally preceded by a period of pronounced professional insecurity. As one might expect, that insecurity is generated by the persistent failure of the puzzles of normal science to turn out as they should. Failure of existing rules is the prelude to a search for new ones.[7]

Science, according to Kuhn, functions as though it "knows what the world is like,"[8] even as throughout history science has been challenged to overcome its presumption of objectivity and recognize its own paradigms.

It seems to me that this "paradigm" talk of Kuhn's hits the nail on the head of current analysis of American Christianity. It seems to me that my struggles as a pastor had at least as much to do with my limiting psychological and theological models of ministry as it did with my particular personality or lack of experience. It seems to me that I was fumbling in ministry because, just as I was entering pastoral work, the phenomenon of church itself was changing. My paradigms were like everyone else's, based upon what our predecessors thought had worked up to that point. I was going through a "pronounced professional insecurity" that was generated by "the persistent failure" of conventional American religious wisdom. It takes this kind of insecurity, according to Kuhn, for new paradigms to spring forth and be tested.

What makes new paradigms for ministry perhaps more challenging is the inability of either seminary or church to "corner the market" on offering any of them, especially in a convincing way. Who has the authority or right to say that this paradigm is inadequate or that one will fill the bill? In one very practical sense, no one does. For some, this admission might seem confusing and disheartening: where do motivated pastors and church people turn for sound direction in times of need? Yet part of the answer has to be that we are in the middle of the paradigm shift itself. The rate and scale of change indeed do stimulate "persistent failure" of old models for ministry. On the other hand, this time of insecurity also frees us to watch for signs of promising fresh paradigms from any sources, whether established or not. Indeed, Kuhn notes that often it is this marginal quality that itself arouses what is necessary to "think outside the box."[9]

Going for the Big Picture

In Kuhn's terms, then, this book offers to the study and practice of parish ministry a shift of paradigms, to the several disciplines of the socials sciences. Such a shift is "new," because it has not been thoroughly utilized; at the same time, it is "old," because it has been marginally available for decades. This book proposes to rename the horseless carriage, by reclaiming the social sciences as a toolbox for ministry, to be the "automobile" beyond the "horseless carriage." This book seeks to promote a new generation of understanding the congregation as a reality in its own right.

As I hopefully have made clear so far, in the actual practice of ministry with congregations, it is my view that the social sciences as a whole have been a neglected companion. It is true that a number of terms from sociology, economics, cultural anthropology, and the like have passed over into American public discourse. For instance, most people have some idea of what phrases like "rites of passage," "middle class," and "role" stand for. However, the *implications* of these concepts for the way that church leaders understand their congregations have yet to be adequately utilized. Thinking social-scientifically opens up a great deal of insight about our congregations that will be both sobering and exciting. Sociology, cultural anthropology, economics, political science, and organizational theory are among the disciplines that offer much to ministry practice and leadership. By learning from, and using, conceptual tools from the social sciences, we are better equipped to create, sustain, and renew congregations.

HEADING IN THE RIGHT DIRECTION

On my way to identifying (oh, so gradually!) the resources in this book, I spent a number of years trying to stay current with what was available and popular. Denominations as a whole did not seem to offer much, but the Alban Institute was very promising. I took seriously the ideas and strategies provided through their growing list of publications. The insights of Loren Mead,[10] Speed Leas,[11] Roy Oswald,[12] Gilbert Rendle,[13] and others have stimulated my thinking and reflection upon what constitutes effective and faithful ministry practice. Although I see the present work as a conceptual shift beyond Alban models, I must acknowledge the contributions that these models and authors have made to my work.

Readers who use this book likely will experience the sensation that accompanies any shift of paradigms. To look at our churches with the lenses of the social sciences helps us see their existence in some significantly new ways. However, we do not have to become anthropologists, for instance, in order to use such conceptual tools in effective ways. Church leaders can develop just as much skill with tools like the ones in this book as American culture already has gained from models and insights from psychology. The main distinction to be made here is the focus upon the congregation, a particular collective human phenomenon that exists over time, and the aim to understand its life, experience, and possibilities.

THE "FAMILY" APPROACH

Many readers will know already that, at the current time, there does exist a popular model for interpreting congregational life. That model is based in a discipline known as "family systems theory," popularized for church audiences through Edwin Friedman's book, *Generation to Generation.*[14] Such a systems model seeks to open up greater insights about congregational dynamics by framing relationships and church behaviors in terms of systems that mirror those among family groups. Proponents of family systems congregational analysis argue that it moves beyond psychoanalytical models. Church members and staff participate in a complex and sometimes confusing system of expectations, behavior patterns, the need for homeostasis, and the like. Church conflicts, proponents further argue, are better understood and managed by understanding the congregation as a system.[15]

It would not be fair to family systems theory as a discipline to attempt in a brief space to spell out its major tenets or critique them. By acknowledging the existence and wide pastoral use of this theory, however, we are better positioned to recognize the context in which the proposal of this book emerges. My impression (and this would need further explication to be accurate or fair) is that family systems theory feels like psychology backing out of a closet and into a room full of the social sciences. "Family systems" appears to offer valuable aid to those who do pastoral care. It might be in over its head when it tries to explain the subtle nuances and intricacies of congregations over time—and what can be done about it. This particular toolbox might not have all of what it takes to help churches with change.

CONGREGATION, REDUX

Churches and change is not a new topic for serious study. Social scientific research on congregations and their environments enjoys a full century of heritage, from centers such as those that emerged in Chicago.[16] Parallel to the well-known "Chicago School" of sociology, with its ecological perspective on urban demographics, the Chicago Theological Seminary developed early field education settings for its parish-bound students. They worked and even lived in settlement houses, learning from Graham Taylor how to think about the sociological dynamics of ministry in a context that changes rapidly. Taylor was succeeded at C.T.S. by Samuel Kincheloe and later Victor Obenhaus; both scholars translated sociological and cultural contexts into insights that seminary students could understand and use.[17]

While this sociological application in theological education maintained a long tradition at the Chicago Theological Seminary, it was not as well known as Paul Douglass' work. Douglass was active with an organization of his day called the Institute of Social and Religious Research. Founded in 1921 and located in New York City, the Institute's goal was to bring research tools from science to bear upon study of religious groups.[18] Douglass authored the

Institute's major study of a thousand Protestant congregations that were located in urban areas.[19] Its interest was in determining what kinds of adjustments the congregations in these cities made in their environments. Their research relied heavily upon statistics, especially of the churches themselves: the report includes more than 120 tables and more than sixty charts. Douglass proposed six types of adaptation[20] and suggested in his conclusions that churches "with changing fortunes or radically fluctuating vision or policy" need to move from one type to another.[21]

Renewed scholarly interest in congregations gave rise in more recent years to a growing, coalescing discipline known as "congregational studies." A new generation of empirical research in American religion has been conducted since the 1970s, by a growing host of well-regarded scholars.[22] Unlike the 1920s emphasis upon statistical data, much of this newer wave of study is ethnographic, centered in telling a congregation's story.[23] Out of this research is being woven a fascinating and very rich tapestry of American congregational life, in all of its diverse forms.

In one sense, the field of congregational studies is a "hard data" version of ideas that James M. Gustafson laid out two generations ago. Gustafson's essay, *Treasure in Earthen Vessels* speaks of "the Church as a human community."[24] In so doing, it opened the way for church people to appreciate the congregation in all its multifaceted complexity. I think of this present work as something of a sequel to Gustafson's. Here the concepts that are presented are more clearly developed and their application demonstrated with actual, pseudonymous congregational stories. Both books find Paul's phrase from 2 Corinthians 4:7 symbolically illuminating: "But we have this treasure in clay jars, so that it may be made clear that this extraordinary power belongs to God and does not come from us." That is, in understanding more clearly and soberly the given realities and limitations of their "clay vessel" conditions, churches can be more forthright and effective about the ways that they recognize and promote God's activity in their midst.

DESIGN AND PURPOSE

Christians historically have found benefit in their ministry to utilize the philosophy and perspectives of their given era. My aim here is no different. As you read a chapter, you will be introduced to descriptions of concepts that then will be narratively illustrated. Often the concepts also can help us to ask the normative questions that flow out of theology: "Is this good? What can we learn from social sciences about our collective human experience that casts a clearer theological light on our human condition? How can this or that concept suggest ways to embrace our theology more fully?" As practical tools, then, the social sciences can reveal to congregations many of the conditions that either prevent or promote their mission. Yet, ultimately, that mission must be expressed and acted out with the language of theology.

Each chapter and each discipline is designed to stand on its own, although readers will detect points where overlap of concepts and themes is evident. Chapter 2 deals with several concepts from sociology. It primary goal is to help the reader make what might at first feel like a quantum leap. Thinking about congregations as congregations leads us to an inevitable qualification of individualism. When individuals congregate, what results is more than the sum of each individual's own experience. Hence, a sound understanding of churches must move beyond the "cocoon syndrome" of the privatizing individualism so prevalent in our era. Categories like "class" and "marginality" make us sit up and take notice of what defines—and often limits—what our congregations do.

Chapter 3 lifts up a number of ways in which congregations express culture. Using terminology borrowed from anthropology, this chapter points out how congregations are driven and defined much more by cultural realities than they are by the cool persuasion of reason. Becoming a leader in the congregation-as-village requires a distinct kind of knowledge and experience that are not automatically granted by joining the church or being called as pastor. Although I find cultural anthropology so illuminating, I deliberately have limited the amount of material in this chapter. Other significant, culturally related concepts and their applications can be found in my earlier books.[25]

Chapters 4 and 5 offer a taste of a congregation's political and economic dimensions. In both chapters, the conceptual framing suggests how choice, participation, and influence in churches grows out of relational dynamics. Market, capital, class, status, party, and governance each depend upon complex and sometimes subtle interactions between persons, structures, and traditions, none of which change easily. These two chapters are shorter than the other three. This is in part because my knowledge of these disciplines is more limited, but also because their application to religious topics in the literature tends to be less extensive.

Chapter 6 presents concepts from *organizational theory* that represent some of the newer thinking in the discipline. In some respects, this chapter integrates material from other chapters, as it lays out a perspective on congregations based on an *open systems* view. Many pastors whom I have met resist the notion that their church is an organization. They prefer to emphasize how Christian theology distinguishes the church from businesses, service agencies, or clubs. Chapter 6 reframes this question so that similarities (of which there are many) and differences (few, but significant) can be perceived more clearly and treated more appropriately. The final chapter returns to general discussion, in seeking to reflect on the relevance of social-scientific tools for ministry practice. Five topics of common interest and concern to many churches today are briefly considered: conflict, governance, religious education, preaching, and renewal/vitality.

Each of the core chapters begins with a true story or situation of a particular congregation that sets the stage for considering the upcoming subject matter. After a few words describing the discipline in general, the form moves back and forth between the concepts and their application to congregations. Then several vignettes or an interpretation of the opening story will suggest how pastors, staff members, officers, and volunteers in such a situation can use the concepts to help them make decisions and lead their churches.

AUTHOR'S LOCATION

This book reflects my interest in and concern for Christian communities of all kinds, although it operates within the parameters of my own experiences and perspective. I grew up in the Pacific Northwest, went to college there, and then received my initial theological education in southern California. After several years of pastoral work in the West, I moved to the Chicago area and ended up staying there for fifteen years. My church staff experience includes United Methodist, Presbyterian, United Church of Christ, and independent traditions; these churches have been small, medium, and large, located in rural areas, small towns, small cities, and Chicago proper. I hold advanced degrees in biblical interpretation and in theology and the human sciences. For five years, I consulted and led training events in several states and regions of the United States. Over the years, I have taught seminary students from Korean, African, European American, Latin American, and African American traditions. At present I teach at a historically African American theological consortium, with six denominations primarily represented and two dozen other Christian expressions among the at-large student constituency.

As a child of the 1960s, I was deeply influenced by the charismatic/evangelical movements of the 1970s, as well as the political and social agendas of the protest movements. I believe that Earth and its inhabitants continue to experience tremendous, sometimes painful and even harmful, changes of many kinds. It is my conviction that congregations of believers who do not actively respond to change eventually will die, sometimes long after they have become irrelevant and have depleted their resources through strife and struggles to survive. Enough has been written in both secular and religious literature in recent years about change and its many effects[26] that I make no attempt here to extend that discussion. It is, however, the backdrop for this book, since change is not going to go away. Tragically, many churches will die because they refuse to see. To those who are willing to look at what is around—and within—them, this book is offered.

CAVEATS AND OPPORTUNITIES

A work of this length and scope cannot elaborate on every nuance of its subject matter. Limiting this discussion, yet finishing with material that will work effectively, was a strenuous endeavor! What I hope to do here is to usher you into a workroom filled with tools, some of which might not be familiar to you. I will contend, however, that, where churches are concerned, it is the workroom of the future. As Whitehead once said, "The vitality of thought is in adventure. . . . Ideas won't keep. Something must be done about them."[27]

I should emphasize as well that I view the discussion in this volume as the beginning of a major conversation, not the final word. Contained herein are concepts, the application of which to congregational ministry makes sense to me. My own pastoral reflections have been more insightful from the vantage point of these ideas. Yet further development of them will be necessary and fruitful. Conceptual identification can be refined and expanded, especially with the topics from those chapters where my knowledge is more limited. Just as importantly, however, will be the work that pastors and others in ministry occupations do to apply these concepts. No doubt we could and might quibble over terms and definitions. Before getting too sidetracked with this kind of scholastic exercise, though, we should encourage readers to focus on use. What difference can these freshly imported disciplines make to ministry practice? If this is the question on your mind when you finish reading this book, I will consider my task to have been successful.

It is my hope and prayer that you will find in these pages ideas to lead you into adventures of faith with your congregation. Read each of the middle chapters as your interest dictates, and ponder the practical significance of these disciplines as you read through chapter 7. And now, let the paradigm-shifting begin!

TWO

BEYOND THE COCOON SYNDROME

Congregation as Social Group

FIELDTOWN AND LORD JESUS CHURCH

On the surface, Fieldtown, U.S.A., looks and acts like many other rural centers that dot the American landscape. For anyone who likes the wide-open spaces and a safe place to raise a family, Fieldtown would fill the bill. Yet, tucked away within the memory of one of Fieldtown's oldest churches is hidden a story of almost unspeakable tragedy. Ironically, the story itself holds clues to the life of this town, this church, and the future of them both.

A modern highway now makes the distances between Fieldtown and its neighbors easier and shorter. For decades, however, this agricultural community led a somewhat sleepy life, even as it slowly grew up, providing more and more homes for those whose occupations supported the small land barons who began farming the area in the late 1800s. Businesses, schools, and professional offices gave

Fieldtown the flavor of a place that offered everything a farm family would need. As people moved in, they also founded churches—places of identity, fellowship, and support for their frontier-like existence.

One of those churches arrived with a particular group of Fieldtown's earliest immigrants. Originally from Europe, these poor farmer families already had been chased out of one hoped-for new home before journeying across the ocean to America. Opportunity, modest as it was, awaited them on the large farms and ranches around the young Fieldtown. These new immigrants worked hard for their bosses, who usually furnished housing for the families on their property. Sunday mornings, wagons brought the families together to worship in their native tongue, share a meal, discuss their work and children, and reminisce about their beloved but distant homeland. Gradually this tightly knit fellowship spawned a formal church for its people.

It was during those first few years of its American experience that this particular community of immigrants endured an incident that spoke so piercingly of their tenuous circumstances.

Two Many Deaths

Because the farms were large and isolated, children of the landowners often ended up playing during the workday with children from the immigrant families. One day, while a group of the children were playing, a landowner's daughter fell into an irrigation ditch that ran between two fields. By the time that adult help could arrive on the scene, the little girl had drowned. When the landowner heard the terrible news, he was so angry that he ordered the immigrant children's family off his property—immediately. So the husband, wife, and children left right away, in great distress.

Deciding to go to one of the other immigrant family's homes, the evacuees painfully shared with their friends the story of the day's tragic events. The husband had had some time to think things over; he decided to go back to the landowner and ask him permission to return to their now-former home and pick up the family's belongings. His wife did not want him to go, knowing how upset the landowner was. But the husband wanted to care for his family. Against her wishes, he traveled back to the farm that day. When the landowner saw him approaching, he got out a rifle and, without warning, shot the immigrant father dead on the spot. Thus a second innocent person died that day. This murder was never prosecuted or investigated.

As the years went by, the clan of immigrants began to prosper. Some of them bought homes in Fieldtown and found employment there; others saved enough money to purchase tracts of land and go into farming for themselves. As the first generation of adults gradually died, more and more of the immigrant families spoke English at home. Their church, Lord Jesus Church, was growing, as first their children and then grandchildren married and started families. It was a proud day after forty years when the congregation broke ground for a brick structure, an ample sanctuary of gleaming woodwork and a balcony with extra rooms for Sunday School and all-church dinners. Not too many years hence, Lord Jesus' elders made the difficult decision to drop their native language in Sunday worship and use only English. By the time their great-grandchildren were being born, the immigrant clan had become full participants in their cozy plains town. The congregation now included farmers, teachers, store owners, and even a state representative. Its horrible memory was fading with the passing years.

Other New Faces

Meanwhile, Fieldtown continued to grow slowly but steadily. A unified school district brought farm and town kids into a larger high school. The new highway was built nearby. Now the grandchildren of the original generation of Lord Jesus Church were aging and dying. The town was changing again, too: it was no longer all white, even though its whiteness was represented by several different European heritages. A new wave of immigration was taking place in Fieldtown and all across the state. These new immigrants had a different color of skin; they spoke a language other than English; they brought with them almost no possessions; they had very few marketable skills; their families were large and poorly dressed. Yet many of their men were able to support families with modest wages earned at the local packing plant—a place where few of the white residents were willing to work.

Members of the Lord Jesus Church noticed Fieldtown's new residents. They noticed that many of the small houses on the street next to their church building were being rented by the immigrant families. The adults spoke broken English; the kids seemed dirty much of the time; on warm days, you could hear strange music being played from their houses. If they attended church, it was at a small one in town that spoke their language. Publicly, Lord Jesus members did not talk about their new neighbors. Privately, one of the trustees wondered aloud if Lord Jesus Church should build a new facility out in one of the new subdivisions.

Every Church

The story of Lord Jesus Church in Fieldtown contains a few elements that are fairly unique to it. After all, not every congregation has lived through the cold-blooded murder of one of its founding members. Yet, the experience of this now well-settled church reveals some things that sound quite similar to the stories of other congregations, too. For churches exist where people are, and people settle and live where they do for a variety of complex reasons. Such factors have been studied by historians, geographers, economists, sociologists, and the like. We tend to take these complex factors that for granted and yet also to acknowledge the part they play in human experience.

This opening chapter seeks to begin to raise our awareness of some of these complex factors of human community. It concentrates on one particular field of study, sociology. Sociology is a broad discipline that includes many approaches, perspectives, and objects of study. It is not our purpose here to summarize all of sociology's basic elements—an impossible task to attempt! Rather, we endeavor to discover how certain particular concepts that have been developed in sociological thought help us understand our churches more fully. The story of Lord Jesus Church in Fieldtown sets the stage. This story affords us an opportunity to ask some significant questions, such as:

- How do the particular stages on which our churches play out their own dramas actually emerge? How can we become more aware of these stages and benefit from this awareness?

- What elements go into creating these stages, their backdrops, scenery, lighting, props, storylines, characters, stars, and so on?

- What do churches have in common among themselves that we might be taking for granted?

- How is the life of a congregation distinguishable from the particular individuals who participate in it?

- What is there about the congregation itself that gives us clues to its own health or its need to adapt?

These are questions that we will begin to answer in this chapter and will pose in other ways in succeeding chapters. They are questions that, unlike many of our American preoccupations, shift our attention away from the experience of individuals.

BEYOND THE COCOON SYNDROME

In other words, a sociological approach to the life of a congregation defines its basic elements beyond private experience. This approach moves in something of a different orbit. I am suggesting in this and subsequent chapters a counter model to the "cocoon syndrome" in American society. We gain a limited kind of insight about our churches if we view them primarily as places for wrapping ourselves up in personal pursuits as priorities.

Religion interacts deeply with the forces of culture and society. As important as modern Western Christianity believes that persons are in the sight of God, it is just as important to realize the ways in which our human experience connects us with others. The field of sociology has provided the twentieth century with an approach to human behavior that puts much of our individual experience in a larger, and quite revealing, perspective. Congregations, their pastors, leaders, and members have much to gain in making their Christian witness effective, by interpreting themselves and their world through a sociological lens. In promoting this claim, I realize that I am emphasizing what many of my colleagues recognize as part of the given landscape around us. What I am suggesting is that we take our social dynamics more deliberately into account and use what we learn, in and for our churches.

A sociological perspective on congregations illuminates the phenomenon of congregational life in some very fundamental and significant ways. This claim will be addressed by introducing several concepts selected from the broad and varied field of sociology. We will look at these concepts in light of what congregations are and do, and also consider some ways that these concepts can help church members and officers act.

A BACKGROUND TO SOCIOLOGY AND RELIGION

Before meeting the concepts themselves, however, it will help us to briefly orient ourselves to the broader study of religion in a sociological perspective. Students of human behavior have noticed a relationship between religion and group experience for a long time. This relationship is rich and complex—perhaps more so than you might imagine.

Togetherness

In looking at religion as a historical phenomenon, we become aware that it virtually always has been deeply grounded in the experience of people being together. Clans and tribes from the most ancient of known times have expressed and enacted spiritual beliefs through activities that are primarily communal. In the Hebrew Bible, the overarching narrative encompassing the earliest chapters of Genesis all the way through the anticipation of Malachi centers on the creation, establishment, dispersion, and restoration of a community. Jesus' ministry, first as he carried it out and later as it was continued by his apostles and other followers, grew out of that same ancient Hebrew/Israelite/Jewish community of old. "Followers of the way" gathered in groups of "called-out ones (ecclesia-church)" for worship, teaching, and support of one another and their ministries. Even the fourth-century monastic movement, in spite of its emphasis upon individual discipline and spiritual nurture, fairly quickly developed communities and traditions to pass on to others.

Classics: Durkheim and Weber

Some of the first modern research in religion was stimulated by interest and method that was sociological. France's Emile Durkheim pioneered many methods, theories, and hypotheses at the turn of the twentieth century. He studied cross-cultural social group behavior and argued that religion played a major role in supporting social stability.[1] In a massive study of suicide statistics in Europe, Durkheim also argued that religion's social influence could be seen in comparing suicide trends among Catholics and Protestants. Suicide rates in heavily Catholic communities were lower than those in heavily Protestant communities. Durkheim argued that Catholic theology places more emphasis upon community than does Reformed Protestantism, with the latter's focus upon the individual's personal spiritual condition before God. Catholics were more likely than Protestants to sense a connection to, and the support of, a social group. Thus, Durkheim concluded that Catholics would be less likely to experience the alienation and despair that can lead some to suicide.

Durkheim's conclusions about the influence of religious tradition upon suicide were considered controversial. His body of work, however, helped to shape a budding discipline and is not the only classical sociological work to have done so—even with religion as its subject. Max Weber, Durkheim's German contemporary, also wrote a considerable amount of his extensive sociological work on relationships between various social institutions and religion. Perhaps most famous is his essay on "The Protestant Ethic and the Spirit of Capitalism."[2] Here Weber made a specific case for the general claim that religious beliefs can influence human institutions, that a society can be affected by the power of particular theological claims. Weber's specific case was the emergence of modern capitalism following the establishment of Reformed Protestant churches in Europe. He argued a somewhat complex case for the Calvinist emphasis upon the mystery of "divine election" as one factor in the belief that accumulation of worldly goods indicated divine favor.

Our purpose here is not to render a judgment on Weber's or Durkheim's conclusions. Instead, we want to acknowledge that more than a century of careful empirical research on connections between religion and collective human behavior lay behind the current generation. To think about religion in sociological terms is not new or unusual.

Theological Sociology

Indeed, as the writings of researchers like Durkheim and Weber became available, they were studied and utilized by Christian scholars, as early as the 1920s. H. Richard Niebuhr's study, *The Social Sources of Denominationalism*,[3] reveals serious and careful appreciation for religion as an expression of human experience that is collective by nature. In this study, Niebuhr was able to show how various Christian traditions in North America related to different social classes over time. His analysis was informed by concepts and methods from Weber. A generation later, James Gustafson published an essay introducing "the church as a human community." This phrase was the subtitle of the 1961 volume, *Treasure in Earthen Vessels*;[4] here Gustafson painted in broad strokes a descriptive outline of the church in its corporate realities. Drawing upon classical sociology as well as organizational theory, he claimed that such perspectives on the church must be utilized along with the normative perspectives of theology.

Gustafson's essay is quite readable and can be very useful to church leaders even today. Yet seminary graduates often are not familiar with it and even less familiar with the practical application of its sociological outlook. The reasons for this lack of awareness are too involved to try to explore here. I am making the point only to emphasize a theme that is implicit throughout this book: that thinking about congregations as phenomena in themselves can yield new insights and action plans that often have remained in the background of what has been our common perspective.

A FEW SOCIOLOGICAL CONCEPTS

Let us now turn to some concepts from the vast field of sociology. These were selected for their ability to help us see churches in a broader framework and then lead them with greater wisdom and confidence.

The Social Group

Human beings live and function in concert with others. This observation might seem trite or all too self-evident, but it is nonetheless still true and still profoundly significant. People do things together, all kind of things, some of which are necessary, some expected, and others selected. In other words, our human connections to community are sometimes given, sometimes spelled out, and other times open to our choice. Perhaps because the twentieth-century West has created so many choices for its inhabitants, we find it more difficult to perceive our human experience as constrained by any natural or contrived factors. They are there, nonetheless, in varying combinations to be sure. Yet no human can escape at least the influence of the social dimension of being human. At this broadest level, we recognize the reality of the social group.

Sociology textbooks often contain a chapter on family, because historically the ways in which humans are born into a group and raised by it have almost entirely determined the experiences and opportunities for all members of that group. Today we also are readily familiar with other kinds of social groups: friends, relatives, coworkers, neighbors, club members, gangs, and the like. Variety of purpose, constituency, activity and general value can, and of course does, vary widely among modern social groups.

One of the offshoots of the general concept of the social group is so important for understanding churches that it will be discussed later in a separate chapter: the organization. The development and proliferation of organizations has been so prevalent that one student of the church and organizational theory comments, "large-scale organizing is the distinguishing characteristic of our contemporary culture."[5] Organization is a special kind of social group, but it also exemplifies many of the qualities of any collective human experience.

The clay jar: a social group. Congregations are a kind of social group. Indeed, the term itself refers to a "getting together," a congregating of persons. Individuals associate and participate with a group that maintains a specific identity, customs, physical and other resources, and so on. This means that, for one thing, a congregation by its very nature does more than simply provide services for individuals. A congregation relates persons to something that is bigger than the sum of all the individuals. I am not referring yet to a theological emphasis; rather, the experience of community that occurs when people participate in a congregation has a life of its own that helps to shape the persons involved.

Weekly worship, study groups, choirs, prayer meetings, sewing circles, potluck dinners, service projects, and the like all create experiences of community. Sociologically, we can argue that such experiences are necessary in order for individuals to create a sense of identity, a perspective on the world and its values, and the motivation and skills to participate in society.

Yet we also know that, for a church, "socializing" is not merely an end in itself. A social-group understanding of congregation is corroborated by biblical and theological images. "People of God" and "the Body of Christ" symbolize a collective unity realized by accepting and participating in God's purposes for creation. It could even be argued that the apostle Paul's understanding of salvation was nowhere near as privatistic as it tends to be interpreted in modern America. His well-known "new creation" passage justifiably could be translated, "If anyone is in Christ, there is a new creation (2 Cor. 5:17)." The sense of Paul's thought here seems to be that individuals join a movement participating with God's aim to reconcile the fallen order through Christ. Rather than implying that salvation becomes a cocoon into which each believer gets comfortably wrapped, this text suggests that salvation calls believers out, into a vocation of overcoming the world's division through sharing the wisdom of elders ("ambassadors"). Such a "social" reading of this text intertwines the spiritual condition of the person and the community tightly together.

Many larger churches on the American scene today recognize the power of the church as a social group in at least one respect. Those who criticize the size of these churches argue that close ties with other human beings is difficult to establish and maintain with hundreds and thousands of persons crowding around you on a Sunday morning. Part of the membership process for many of these churches is immediately to involve new members in some kind of small-group fellowship. In some regular fashion, new members meet in groups of six to twelve. They might share a meal, study a biblical text, intercede in prayer for others in need, or the like. Within this setting, church leaders deliberately design opportunities for these new members to know others, become known, to share something of themselves and the value of their lives. While such activities might be designed primarily to feed individual needs, they also create bonds that are associated with a social group. The congregation becomes a place not simply for one's personal salvation but, as part of being "in Christ," also fellowship, learning, helping, and serving. In this way, the faith for which the congregation exists is expressed and nurtured because of a social group.

The Voluntary Association

Not all social groups allow their members to choose whether or not they belong. In this era, however, we have become very familiar with a kind of group that is prized perhaps more than any other in the freedom-loving United States. This hybrid concept of social group and organization was identified decades ago by the likes of Weber and later explored extensively from several angles by James Luther Adams. This concept takes form under political conditions that permit individuals to choose to band together for either pleasure or public task.[6] It is called the concept of voluntary association.

"Voluntary association" sounds simple at first, yet its purposes, forms, and effects can be, and indeed are, vastly diverse. As a historical phenomenon, voluntary associations emerged significantly in the West during the Protestant Reformation (especially through its radical, Anabaptist wing) and have proliferated to a staggering degree in the twentieth century. They range from freely elected governments to fan clubs and, more recently in our home computer age, Internet groups. The key characteristics are the freedom of individuals to choose to associate, which in turn is possible because of a form of government that does not force membership or participation in particular groups.

A simple way to illustrate the historical distinctiveness of the development of the voluntary association is by asking yourself to think of your opinion about an issue such as gay rights or funding for public education. Then call to mind the groups or coalitions of which you have heard that advocate the position that you oppose! They are allowed to exist because the United States government does not ban freedom of expression or groups who disagree with each other. In this illustration, the associations are *instrumental*, in that they seek to influence behavior in the public arena. Perhaps even more extensive are those voluntary associations that are *expressive*, that is, serving various desires that members seek to meet for enjoyment.[7] In either type, the existence of voluntary associations at the scale with which we now experience them is historically fairly new.

Youth soccer leagues, book clubs, fraternal organizations, scouting groups, hobby associations—and churches!—are all voluntary associations. In spite of differences that appear on the surface, their basic common features involving freedom of activity, structure, participation, and governance have defined a form of social group that is historically somewhat unique. The influence of the voluntary association upon modern life cannot be underestimated.

Church—by choice. Not only are churches social groups, but in the modern world they are less imposed upon persons than they are chosen. The influence of America's tradition of voluntary associations on the religious scene is difficult to overestimate. Most people tend not to realize that their very option in selecting religious association—not to mention other basic factors such as residence, education, occupation, and recreation—is a given option. Certainly it is true that most religious traditions try to encourage loyalty. Some, like Roman Catholic traditions, have been able to maintain more members, in part due to ethnic and cultural ties as much as due to religious loyalty.[8] But the changing nature of American culture in general has created an atmosphere in which few religious groups can simply assume that new members will join and current members will remain.

Churches who realize the social and voluntary nature of their existence will pay attention to both of these characteristics, in proactive ways. As we already have seen, a number of today's churches deliberately involve their new members in small groups. These experiences meet needs for developing personal relationships and fostering spiritual growth, to be sure. Through such experiences, persons in small groups strengthen their loyalty to the church as a whole, particularly if small-group goals are consistent with the congregation's.

Of greater challenge to today's churches is to maintain membership participation so that members do not drop out of sight and eventually out of church. This issue is difficult to address on its own, without discussing the role played by a congregation's vision. One growing church sends out a form to every member annually. The form is to be sent back, indicating whether the person chooses to be a member for another year. In this way, the person's decision to actively express his or her faith in a community of faith is kept before that person regularly. The other side of this practice points to the nature of the church. It is a group that depends upon the decision of individuals. It exists by voluntary association.

Movement and Institution

A third concept from sociology that will help to illuminate the realities of churches is actually a pair of concepts. This pair has been described by a number of sociologists[9] who have observed a certain similarity of phenomena in social groups. They note that groups can be differentiated in part along a continuum of style and function. Some groups are more enthusiastic, less structured, driven by a key leader, and more flexible. Many of these groups tend to be just a few years old. Other groups, often having existed for many years, exhibit more stability and structure, less energy, and participants who maintain tried-and-true activities and practices. This continuum has been variously called "liminal and differentiated," "emergent and established," "effervescent and ritualistic." Here we will use the terms "movement" and "institution."

Max Weber understood these two concepts implicitly as he distinguished between forms of authority.[10] He employed the term "charisma" to speak of the influence commanded by a focused, convicted, energetic person whose message and way of life initiate some kind of new movement. In spite of any success that the new movement might have, inevitably it must face the matter of survival without its charismatic founder. Movements that do survive, therefore, must make a transition from the leader's personal authority to a "routinization" of that charisma. Such routinization changes the character of the movement, as it begins to institutionalize its activity and processes in order to maintain itself indefinitely. This ongoing maintenance then takes on either "traditional" authority—as it has in most of history—or "bureaucratic" authority—as we have seen most evidently in the last century.

Throughout our own past generation, the basic differences between movements and institutions at times have been painfully evident. The "anti-establishment" youth movement in the 1960s opposed the behavior of highly institutionalized, complex groups; often multinational corporations, the armed forces, or governmental bodies were targeted. Those of us who were in churches during these years know that "the youth movement" had negative things to say about the church's "irrelevance."

This same generation of cultural unrest also saw significant new forces in American religion emerge. A "charismatic movement" swept through all established church traditions. Hundreds of ecumenical prayer groups met in churches, homes, and restaurants across the country. Participants read the Bible; listened to lay speakers interpret it; prayed silently, aloud, and "in tongues"; and sought to revitalize congregations that they perceived to be stodgy, rigid, and only marginally Christian. During the same time period, the evangelical Protestant tradition surged into prominence, making its mark in congregational resources, literature, music, television and video media, journalism, and even politics.

These observations lead us to ask, Why have so many parachurch groups that are evangelical still going strong, while charismatic groups have dissipated and mainline churches continue to struggle? The same question can be posed in the secular arena of society: why do some fads like break-dancing fizzle out fairly quickly, while others like rap music remain popular? Part of the answer to this vital question lies in understanding the concepts of movement and institution.

Mendocino as movement and institution. R. Stephen Warner's sociological study of a small-town church does not answer all the questions posed above, but it certainly helps to validate their importance. Warner reports how the well-established, quiet, and staid Mendocino Presbyterian congregation began in the early 1970s to get involved with a hippie commune. Through the efforts of a "fellowship" including a few new and evangelically minded church members, the commune became converted. Many of the commune residents then joined the Presbyterian church while maintaining participation in the fellowship. These "evangelical" church members then were able to influence the selection of the congregation's next pastor, himself evangelical. In the ensuing years, the Mendocino congregation saw dramatic increases in worship attendance, official membership and per member giving, even though the town was not growing and their denomination was losing members.

This story sounds like a dream come true, but the church also experienced its contests. Decisions about style of worship, programming, and mission activity had to be negotiated between church old-timers and the enthusiastic newcomers. Eventually, the primary evangelical lay leader left over various disputes. Warner argues that the evangelical movement in the Mendocino church succeeded in certain respects, but the institutional side of the congregation won out in other ways. While movements generate considerable energy, institutions create a staying power that, in the long run, often thwarts a movement's goals.

A Legacy of Cultural Unrest

Mendocino Presbyterian Church exemplifies many of the issues over movement and institution that were quite apparent on the American scene in the 1960s and 1970s. The many new, high-energy, informal, and often short-lived religious groups of that era expressed the concept of movement quite well. Thousands of people during those years participated in groups like these. Organs and pianos were replaced by guitars and drums; group singing often consisted of music so new that much of it was not copyrighted; people stood up and spoke freely about their struggles in life and how their faith helped them. Someone would do some "teaching" on a biblical text. There was a tremendous energy built up in these gatherings, which contrasted starkly with the formalities of most church worship at the time. Since many of those attending these new Christian meetings grew up with church experience, there was no question which style and emphasis they preferred.

Church back home, by contrast, often exemplified most of the features of institutionalism. It maintained its many traditions, hardly concerned about the religious hurricanes blowing down the streets. Familiar activities and routines continued year after year, with the same coterie of participants. Members of these churches tended to believe that the viewpoints of "those young people" eventually would turn around, once they got a little older and settled down to work and raising families. Then they would come back to church.

Today, a generation later, many of the churches back home are smaller in size than they were; some, after years of painful struggle, have closed their doors. Meanwhile, most of those youth-oriented gatherings have disappeared, although a few of them have become full-fledged congregations, with several services a week and a plethora of educational, fellowship, and outreach activities. These contrasts, between two very different kinds of religious communities, illustrate the phenomenon of movement and institution.

Neibuhr's early schema. Warner's sociological study of one specific congregation continues a long scholarly tradition of applying concepts like movement and institution to corporate religious expression. Niebuhr's study of church and class mentioned earlier[11] promoted three terms to describe changes in religious character and style. The *sect* phase corresponds to the concept of movement—focus, enthusiasm, discipline, dynamic, single authority, and so on. The second phase, *church*, would be somewhere between movement and institution. It displays some of the enthusiasm and discipline of the sectarian period but also has developed processes for continuity and close associations with like-minded local bodies. The third phase, *denomination*, represents a historical, Christian form of the generic sociological concept of institution. Layers of relationships—local, regional, and national—become well-defined; conviction and enthusiasm tend to be replaced by tolerance and propriety; leadership is characterized by supporting the group's stated purposes and goals.

Both Warner and Niebuhr suggest that a congregation's social structures and general tone go through some fundamental changes over a period of time. Religious groups that, in their early years, generate strong conviction, high levels of commitment, a sense of being set apart for special work, often through the singular influence of a dynamic leader—such groups do not maintain themselves in that style indefinitely. If they survive past the death of the founding figure, they do so because of two key adjustments. One is in the particular focus, which usually becomes less rigid and severe. The other is in setting up structures and processes to maintain the group's life. Inevitably this institutionalization means that the religious group loses its original, self-defined cutting edge, seeking instead to coexist with its world at large. Although this phenomenon occurs in any long-lived religious group, in American history it has been most notable among the traditions of mainline Protestantism.

Indeed, one way to interpret church history is by noting the various movements that arise as a response to perceived lack of faithfulness by the dominant religious institution. Then, as time goes by, the same movements that protested the spiritual conditions of the day gradually take on similar qualities themselves! Since the right to choose religion is upheld by the United States Constitution, North America has become in many ways a grand experiment in religious pluralism. In other words, the voluntary nature of most religious groups in the United States promotes a fertile soil for a cycle of new religious movements and their eventual demise or institutionalization.

Role

A young pastor in one of my seminary courses recounted an incident that he had experienced in his first pastoral appointment. Following the first Sunday's worship service, the congregation's members filed past Rev. Walker, politely greeting him and shaking hands. In the line, ahead of his mother, was a bright-looking five-year-old. Before his mother had a chance to say anything, the young lad looked Rev. Walker in the eye and exclaimed, "My momma says you may be our preacher, but you ain't our pastor yet!"

As humorous and embarrassing as this anecdote might have been at the time, it nonetheless illustrates a general human phenomenon that is commonly overlooked and underappreciated. Human beings exist in multiple, social relationships. These relationships at times conflict with each other; in some societies (as in the United States), these relationships can change. The concept used to describe the behavior of persons in certain relationships is called "role."

In the minds of member's of Rev. Walker's first parish, the role of preacher was not automatically equated with that of pastor—although we might want to argue both roles ideally should reside in the same person. The same observation is true outside of the church as well. Any society tends to impose expectations for patterns of behavior that are associated with various recognized roles. Since American society has developed such a premium upon individual freedom, we have seen in recent history an increasing struggle between individuals and the roles that they take on while seeking to move beyond society's traditional expectations. Gender stereotypes in employment offer one of the most dramatic and persistent forms of contemporary role struggles. Women who seek jobs and careers in traditionally male areas of employment face the challenge of being convincing in the job, doing it well, and maintaining their own sense of identity.

George Bernard Shaw's play *Pygmalion* (and its musical version, *My Fair Lady*) reveals several broad features about role, for men and women, and in a society that was fairly rigid but has been modified by individualism. Professor Higgins does not see Eliza Doolittle as anything more than an object of his expertise and persistence. Not only do her working-class background and manners work against her, but Eliza is also a woman in an England during which few opportunities were available to women, even those with means. When Eliza attends the ball and leaves the impression on the unknowing guests that she is an exotic princess, something stirs within her. It has something to do, of course, with wanting Professor Higgins to acknowledge her as a human being with feelings and desires. Yet her yearning also takes on a sociological dimension: she wants to change roles. No more ignorant flower girl for her! Eliza is ready to become something of a "lady."

The potential flexibility of role in a church can be illustrated by the story of Ted. Ted was baptized, raised, and confirmed in the same church and kept his membership there during college. Returning home to begin his professional career, Ted remained active in his home church. Some years later, he sensed a call to parish ministry, completed a seminary degree, and then was hired as an associate pastor for his home church. Ted had played several roles in his church throughout his lifetime—newborn, baptized, child, youth, confirmed, college student, young businessman, student again, pastoral staff. Perhaps none of these roles has been as dramatic a shift as becoming one of his church's pastors. Being an associate, however, Ted's pastoral role did not involve the kind of responsibility and status accorded the church's head of staff, which for many members is viewed as the pastoral position. Ted then could still maintain certain ties to his church in a way not too different from his younger years. The chances were good that Ted's pastoral role in his home church would work fairly comfortably and effectively.

I am what I do? The place of the sociological notion of "role" in individual experience has a tendency in today's modern society to be overlooked. Sometimes, personal struggles that are often labeled by popular thinking as "inner" conflicts originate in a social setting. A person's can feel confusion about various actual and possible roles in a society that at least on the surface permits a wide range of role selection.

Hilda was a contented mother who worked capably for years in the family business. As her youngest child reached junior high, Hilda felt restless. She and her family had always been active in their church, but Hilda sensed a desire in herself to do more. Ordination seemed to be calling her. So she enrolled in college to begin a seven-year process of educational preparation for pastoral ministry. Her denomination did not ordain women, but the matter was under considerable debate and Hilda was optimistic about the timing. She studied, continued to volunteer at church, graduated from college, began seminary, completed field education requirements, and did some supply preaching. When she received her seminary degree, Hilda's denomination was still fighting over the question of women's ordination.

Although a pleasant and gracious person, Hilda admitted to her friends that the ordination matter was hard on her. For generations, her family had been part of their church tradition. She felt a call to ordained ministry, but the path was blocked by church politics. It seemed almost inconceivable to Hilda to switch denominations. More than once during weekly chapel services her final year at seminary, Hilda's eyes filled with tears. More than once, her voice would break as she updated classmates on her ordination ordeal. Here was a mature and gifted person, ready to take on a special role that was denied her. The pain was evident—the pain of trying to fulfill a role for which Hilda was well-prepared.

Hilda's experience with role changes is not that unusual these days. When family, job, and church used to be seen as fairly straightforward decisions for young adults, their roles came easier. In an era when many stereotypes are dissolving, where economic forces do not guarantee lifelong careers with one company, where mobility is still high, and where ethical and religious values have also become pluralistic, the matter of one's role in the world takes on a paramount, but tottering, significance.

Status

When Michael Jordan was cut from his high school basketball team at the age of fifteen, the only people who would have shown much interest in him were his family, some friends, and perhaps a teacher or two. When Jordan went to the University of North Carolina to play basketball, probably many residents of his hometown paid attention. When he helped his team win a national championship, thousands of basketball fans across the country took notice—and so did the professional scouts. When Jordan signed with the Chicago Bulls, Nike shoes took a chance that the rookie's play and personality would help the company sell shoes. When Jordan came out of retirement a decade later, the excitement in Chicago was like electricity in the air.

Michael Jordan's athletic career illustrates yet another useful concept from sociology: that of "status." Simply defined, status is *a relative position of esteem or regard accorded to individuals by society or a group in society*. What creates the esteem or regard? Many factors can and do contribute to it. Take Jordan's status and analyze its factors. One, of course, is that he is extremely skilled and competitive in a sport that millions of people love to watch. Another factor could be his natural good looks: Michael Jordan makes an appealing presentation in front of a camera. But probably what contributes just as much to Jordan's status is that he is usually perceived as a gentleman, a really nice guy. Mix all this together, and you have superstardom, a highly visible and high-status phenomenon.

We should be careful to realize, however, that not all status is positive, nor is it always possible to earn. Traditionally, status came "with the territory," that is, with the position in life that one's family maintained in their society. This kind is usually called *ascribed* status. Children of royalty enjoy higher status than those of mine workers. As we will see below, status is often—but not entirely— linked with class. Sometimes in a nation or community a person with ethical or spiritual fortitude can become a hero of sorts, in symbolizing values and behavior dear to the community. Although Billy Graham's theology does not personally attract the vast majority of Americans, Graham often has made the annual list of America's top ten most admired men.

Similarly, status ranges on a scale from high to low. Another American sports hero, O. J. Simpson, achieved high status as a college and professional football player. Years after this retirement, Simpson maintained a regular stream of product endorsements and acting parts, until his ex-wife and her friend were murdered. Suspicion over his possible role in their deaths developed to a level that his endorsement contracts were cancelled; his ability to symbolize a wholesome, trustworthy person had been tarnished, perhaps for the rest of his life. In some arenas of the public eye (but certainly not to everyone), Simpson's status has fallen from respectable to questionable.

Both O. J. Simpson and Michael Jordan illustrate the other kind of status, the one that has become much more possible today because of the combination of political, economic, and social factors at work in the world. *Achieved* status arises when a person does something that a social group recognizes as meeting of one its implicit or explicit criteria. Education, athletic achievement, career upward mobility, and newly acquired wealth are some of America's more easily recognizable contributors to achieving a higher status. Crime and ethical/moral violations often (but not always!) trigger movement to a lower status.

Status also operates with different symbols for different social groups in a society. Gang signs are regarded very differently among the gang itself, the community, and law enforcement agencies. Clothing and hairstyles tend to be major symbols of status among Western youth, but the same items usually do not carry the same status for adults. Thus, determining what operates in what social group, and in what manner, as status-evoking becomes a fascinating—and sometimes confusing!—question.

Status in biblical narrative. Status changes can be found frequently in the Bible. Abram left the security of his parents' urban setting (higher) to travel and wander through the desert with all his family and belongings (lower) (Gen. 12:ff). Joseph, Jacob's eleventh son, rode something of a status roller coaster during his lifetime

(Gen. 37–50). As a favorite of his father (high), Joseph ended up being sold by his brothers to a caravan. Sold in Egypt, Joseph became a slave (low) in the household of an army captain. When he refused advances from the captain's wife, Joseph was accused of rape and thrown into prison (very low). His ability to interpret dreams accurately led to Joseph's appointment by the pharoah to be governor over all Egypt (very high), to prepare for a famine. Once the famine took hold, Joseph's brothers traveled to Egypt to buy food (low). When Joseph finally revealed his identity to the brothers, they feared retribution, even though Joseph arranged for the entire clan to relocate to a desirable region of Egypt. Joseph's high status permitted him to save his clan—and the saga of the people of God continued.

There are other such narratives in the Bible that indicate changes in public esteem among key characters: Moses, Rahab the harlot, Ruth, David, and, of course, Jesus and Paul. The presence within these stories of movement in the character's status indicates that the phenomenon itself has been recognized by human communities for epochs. It also suggests that status becomes a factor in theological thinking and in religious community.

Status in and with Congregations. It would be virtually impossible to argue that status plays no part in the life of congregations! Indeed, the "earthen-ness" of our church vessels is expressed in their awareness of status as much as any other factor. There are a number of ways that we can see status at work in a congregation; these include the pastoral role, certain elected positions, persons whose outside status affects their regard by the congregation, status of the congregation in the community, varying statuses of congregations among other religious organizations, and the like.

In the previous section on role, we saw how Ted's role in his home church changed several times over the years, especially when he became one of its pastors. Changes in role often lead to changes in status. Hence, when we consider one sociological concept as it relates to churches, we almost inevitably engage others as well.

Class

Human social experience is not driven simply by public regard for certain attitudes and behavior. Matters of status sometimes can be shaped more by a sense of what is considered right and good than by daily realities. In most of history, such realities have been strongly determined by another phenomenon, one that sociology has identified and named.

Class describes the varied positions of particular kinds of people that are created by economic opportunity and achievement.[12] It has become commonplace in our time to speak of roughly three classes—upper, middle, and lower—although sociologists and economists can break this division down even further. Upper-class persons maintain the most wealth and property, which is often inherited. Middle-class persons maintain their class standing, with its opportunity for increasing material possessions and options, through a combination of educational preparation and income through employment. Lower-class persons struggle with minimal income, low-skilled jobs that pay modestly, and little chance for improving their situation. In speaking of "the American Dream," we refer to the compelling notion that anyone could emigrate to the United States, start out at the bottom, and succeed in gaining substantial material wealth.

Indeed, the very fact that a conversation about the realities and complexities of class can occur daily in the public arena of newspapers and television points to a peculiar development of historical factors. For most of human experience, the vast majority of persons and communities have lived in hardly more than a survival, peasant-type mode. On a world scale, this is still often the case, although the presence of a large middle class (of sorts) in North America and Europe tends to mislead us.

Class has been a major factor in virtually all known civilizations. Commonly, a very small ruling class was supported by a slightly larger class of administrators, merchants, and artisans. The life and work of both rulers and their immediate supporters was justified and maintained by edict, law, and economic patterns. As a result, the largest part of any population survived in a subservient position of illiteracy and menial labor. Perhaps the most observable version of a class system today is in India, with its four-thousand-year-old caste system. As with most class structures, this complex system—with its four basic castes and hundreds of subcastes—has been legitimated by religious belief and circumscribes an individual's entire life activity. Violations of caste are serious offenses with attendant consequences: Mohandas Gandhi himself was "excommunicated" from his own caste for disobeying its rule of not leaving India (as a young man, he traveled to England to study law).

Because class plays such a pivotal role in social power, it will be considered further in chapter 5.

The classy church. As a sociological reality, class influences congregations. Class probably influences congregations more than most earnest Christians would like to admit. When we are aware of how class functions in society, we also become aware of some measure of tension that it creates with the welcoming proclamation of the Christian gospel. Yet, most of our towns and neighborhoods tend to have churches that reflect the varying classes within their bounds. A pastoral colleague of mine once remarked to me that laborers and small business owners did not feel comfortable going to the same church as their doctor, their lawyer, and their banker.

These distinctions are very familiar to most of us—as perhaps also are the discomforts! People have a tendency to want to associate with others "like themselves," and economic condition easily ranks as one of the categories of "being like us." In many of America's older towns, the difference between church class is often observable simply by location. Churches close to the downtown area often are well-established and higher class than churches on the edge of town. As the economic level of a particular part of town changes, however, so often does that of the church. Next time you go driving through a town or city, notice where the churches are and which ones suggest which kind of status.

Marginality

The last concept which we will consider in this chapter is one that does not receive quite as much attention in sociology textbooks as do the others mentioned. As we will see, however, it is a concept that not only has relevance for sociology; but it also can speak profoundly in a theological way, too. This is the notion of a person or group being perceived, or perceiving oneself, as somehow on the edge of the overall community. Persons or groups who experience themselves as not fitting in—or who are treated this way—are considered marginal.

Marginality is a concept that can be applied in just about any sociological situation, since its definition allows it to cut across other sociological categories. For instance, marginality is one way to describe the position of ethnic minority groups in a country.

North America in the seventeenth century was populated primarily by native tribes who, by the nineteenth century, had become a minority, as were the African slaves on southern American plantations. One of my brothers moved to Japan as a young man and has spent most of his life there, marrying a native woman of the country and raising two children while pursuing a career. Even though he speaks Japanese fluently, he is a Euroamerican; he experiences Japanese life somewhat differently than the Japanese do; he is perceived—because of his race and origin—as a minority person. At the same time, my brother can visit the United States and "fit right in," at least on the surface!

Within the United States, marginality has become an implicit social agenda in the ongoing civil rights movement. Marginality is not defined only by skin color, nation of origin, how much money one makes, whether a person is male or female, or similar parameters. Race, class, gender, age, and sexual orientation all have become national issues. What they have in common is the conviction that the marginality that each category tends to foster is not right and should be eliminated from the public arena—education, housing, employment, and so on. As important as each one of these civil rights movements is, however, they do not exhaust the ways in which the concept of marginality can be utilized.

My guess is that even many white, educated, well-employed males—the traditional stereotype of social acceptability and opportunity—could identify at least one way in which they do not completely "fit in." I was born an identical twin, and both of us are left-handed. Neither one of these factors might seem significant to persons who are not twins and not left-handed, but my brother's and my experience suggests otherwise. In our growing-up years, we were treated differently from the other children. We were constantly being compared to each other; we had to learn how to write, use scissors, and throw a ball on our own, because our teachers were not sure how to show us the left-handed way. Sometimes we liked the "extra" attention; other times it turned out not so positive. Either way, there were times when we stuck out, and we knew it.

Researchers who have interviewed persons who rescued Jews from Nazi attack during World War II have identified as one key characteristic that rescuers shared the notion of "social marginality."[13] For some of the rescuers, the marginality was in being Roman

Catholic in a Protestant community, or the other way around. For others, it was that they were in a position of influence and/or wealth. Whatever the factors were, rescuers recognized those factors as having an effect on their view of themselves and the events surrounding Nazism and the war. When situations presented themselves, these persons could empathize with the threatened Jews; that empathy helped them to take risks to their own lives in order to protect innocent persons from harm.

Because marginality does not function in the same way as status or class, it is in some respects a more elusive concept to utilize easily or favorably. Marginality is also a category that is difficult to sustain in specific situations over long periods of time. Many persons and communities who recognize in themselves some kind of marginality seek to overcome it. Being different is not popular. Yet being different can also, in certain times and places, be useful and helpful. By lifting up this concept, we can become more aware of situations in which marginality is at work. Such awareness then can enhance one's ability to engage proactively in a worthwhile enterprise.

Biblical marginality. Marginality can be an insightful way to interpret many persons and events in the Bible. Status changes to which we alluded above for Joseph and Moses left them marginal much of their lives—whether in the bulrushes, prison, or wilderness, or in the palace or at the head of the wilderness procession. Several female characters rose from obscurity to play significant roles in acting out the faith to which the Israelites were called. Jesus came from Nazareth of Galilee—a very marginal region of his day—to an eventual death by Roman crucifixion—a most marginal way to die.

Leaning on the edge. If honest recognition of class and status cause many churches to feel at least a twinge of theological discomfort, then marginality is the concept for putting that discomfort on a backspin. In other words, marginality can be used as a proactive and positive approach to framing a congregation's posture in its life and community. For most congregations, this is traveling new territory, but it can help to energize a church as part of a renewed vision of its identity and purpose.

When the concept of marginality is used to help interpret stories and persons from the Bible, a congregation increases its likelihood that it will locate ways that it could develop its own marginality in theologically sound ways. As noted earlier, biblical characters such as Joseph (of "coat of many colors" fame), Moses, and Jesus can be understood in greater theological relief when the implications of their own marginalization are explored.

This is a claim that needs more space to spell out than is available here, so a brief explanation will have to point out the direction of thought. In all three cases, part of the wonder of their stories rests in the unlikely conditions of their lives. A young, bragging nomad boy becomes second-in-command in Egypt and saves his family (Joseph). A slave's son is raised in the palace, flees his royal life, and returns as a shepherd to demand release of the king's slaves (Moses). A backwater Jew excites peasants with his preaching, teaching, and healing (Jesus). Their marginality made Joseph, Moses, and Jesus implausible heroes, but it also gave them a creative edge over conventionality. Theologically, these narratives suggest a notion that becomes a theme in the Bible: "Look what amazing things God can accomplish through unexpected people!"

The apostle Paul is another case in point. Remember that marginality does not have to mean only "being on the bottom;" often well-placed and wealthy persons live on the edge of their communities, too. Being both a Pharisee and a Roman citizen, Paul maintained official high status among his ethnic community as well as in the ruling empire. Yet, in his Christian ministry, he uses both points of status almost as foils. Paul says that, if he seeks to impress anyone, he will do so on the basis of the beatings, stonings, accusations, and traveling dangers that he endured as an apostle for Christ: "If I must boast, I will boast of the things that show my weakness" (2 Cor. 11:30). The ability to see himself as different helped Paul with both strength and vision for his work.

Making the most of marginality. In the wake of American civil unrest precipitated during the 1960s, the young, urban, middle-class, black True Spirit Church saw its membership drop from two hundred to eighty. Although surrounded by thousands of other African Americans in their part of the city, this congregation was struggling for a viable ministry. Their pastor resigned, and the church appointed a search committee. That committee did something courageous: they prepared a statement to guide pastoral selection. Agreeing that the church needed to serve its black community as a black congregation, the committee sought a pastoral candidate who would help develop this vision.

Their clarity of search paid off. The congregation approved a youthful, well-educated candidate with a dynamic style of leadership. Within a matter of a few years, it was clear that the new direction was right on target. Their worship added drums and contemporary-style singing; the pastor preached without a manuscript. Persons were challenged to decide about faith in Christ. The congregation grew, adding services, ministry activities, and hundreds more members.

Yet there was something else that grew out of True Spirit Church's new vision, something that was integral to these increases. What guided the development of ministry was a conviction about the church's view of black Christianity in the wider culture. The pastor encouraged education and getting good jobs, but he articulated a different goal than the popular view of "grabbing all the gusto you can get." Instead, the church takes its ethnic marginality and turns it into a motivator for Christian life and witness. "Don't get sucked into the world's game of power and possessions," the church teaches its youth. "The sinful nature of society's dominant power does not really want us, anyway. So use your talents, your education, your income to do ministry for Africans and African Americans, in the name of Christ."

Today, True Spirit Church has become well-enough known that it has been written up in the local newspaper. It has a larger facility now, to accommodate its more than sixty outreach programs. A number of its members have gone on to seminary and become ordained pastors and church workers. One of the associate pastors took a contingent of the present congregation to establish a second congregation in a suburban area. What is the "secret" of their success? There are no secrets to dynamic Christian witness. Yet it becomes clear that this congregation has been able to reach more people and do more in its community because it took its own type of marginality (in this case, racial) and turned it on its head. Churches who can see themselves as somehow on the edge of things, who can develop a productive vision out of that "borderlike" awareness, are thus poised to create exciting, positive opportunities for living and sharing Christian faith.

LORD JESUS CHURCH AND FIELDTOWN: A SOCIOLOGICAL ANALYSIS

Lord Jesus Church today bears a long story, partly told and partly untold, revealing in varying degrees the sociological features that we have been discussing. It is a social group originally founded as a voluntary association in its homeland. Its movementlike convictions led it to seek opportunity first in one nation and then, after being driven out, in young America. Faith and religious practice kept the immigrants together. They endured marginality and tragedy in the first years of American settlement. Over the decades, their class and status in Fieldtown gradually rose to middle-class characteristics. Some features of their congregational life became institutionalized along the way. Every one of their pastors, except the most recent one, has been of the same ethnic heritage as the original immigrants. That was a role that was hard for the congregation to change.

Much of Lord Jesus' story could be the story of hundreds of other congregations in North America. What do these several concepts suggest about Lord Jesus' future and, indirectly, about other congregations,' too? Let us consider this question as we elaborate upon this sociological outlook.

One of the ways that religious groups in North America became established was through migration as particular communities. Mennonites, Presbyterians, Roman Catholics, Jews, and many others entered the New World not simply as immigrants, but also as people of faith. They intended to make their faith and church a central element of their new life. And, not infrequently, they migrated together. The immigrants who founded Lord Jesus Church were a social group that (at least during one point in time) depended for its existence upon the voluntary association of men and women from their native land. Those who came to America chose to come, in this case to come together, and to come because of their religious ties. Since the political environment of the United States tolerated voluntary association of religion, Lord Jesus Church had a chance to survive and thrive.

Lord Jesus Church had gained its original vision and energy from a movement in its homeland. This movement had begun as a protest against the state church and its lack of spiritual vitality. Anyone who joined this movement discovered soon enough that the stakes were fairly high. There was no guarantee that adherents would receive government protection. Neighbors, and even former friends, could make life difficult or even dangerous. By the time that this band of families settled in the States, their ethnic heritage lent additional strength to their identity and commitment. Their cause was economic, political, and religious freedom.

After a number of decades, Lord Jesus Church showed signs of having become an institution. Its membership was aging and few younger members were joining. The women's society worried that the younger women would not take over their quilting project that had been maintained for sixty years. The building needed some maintenance that was somewhat expensive. When they called, for the first time, a pastor without the same ethnic heritage as the congregation, an institutionalized role had been redefined. A few older members were quietly concerned. The question was whether that particular change in pastors, symbolic for the congregation, would signal other changes, too.

Members of Lord Jesus by and large had become well-accepted and comfortable residents of the Fieldtown area. This was evident at their centennial celebration: people dressed in suits, ties, dresses, and shiny shoes; the parking lot held a number of Buicks and Cadillacs; several civic figures attended the ceremonies. Children of multigenerational Lord Jesus members were active in their schools, watched television, listened to music like their peers and liked to go shopping at the mall in Bigtown, an hour's drive away. As a community, Lord Jesus Church members were no longer marginal, lower-class, and lower-status. You could pick few of them out of a crowd; they had assimilated into the mainstream of American society.

Perhaps their assimilation contains a hint of inherent duplicity. On the one hand, Lord Jesus Church moved with mild misgivings to call its first nonethnic pastor. This symbolic link to their origins was difficult to give up. On the other hand, the former immigrant community had assimilated sufficiently to miss identifying with the marginalized condition of its new neighbors. It was not just time that faded the early memories, but also their upward movement in class and status, along with institutionalization that was now evident in church practice.

Eric Thomas, Lord Jesus' new pastor, intuitively picked up on these congregational characteristics. Young and thoughtful, this new pastor had enough experience to show respect for the congregation's background and traditions. However, he also wanted the church to keep its faith alive and fresh and its outreach responsive to community needs. He especially wondered how this congregation felt about the town's latest wave of immigrants.

As part of a renewal training project, a team of Lord Jesus' church leaders gathered stories among the congregation about the church's heritage. The team heard from one of its older members for the first time the story of the girl who drowned and the immigrant father who was murdered. It was a story that all the old-timers knew but had never shared publicly. When the team reported the story during one of the training meetings they were asked an important question: How could their church's own history of being oppressed immigrants help them discover ministry to the town's newest immigrants?

It was a question that arose more than once during the training and that this team of lifelong church members and new pastor Thomas did not "jump on" right away. Yet, it was a question that found its way into a new declaration of vision that the team eventually prepared and even shared with other church members, to a favorable response. The work to deal with old attitudes of class and status, role and marginality, still lay ahead of the team and the church. For the first time in its history, however, this congregation was in a position to name something new about itself. The shoe was on the other foot now, but the church could choose to make a difference. Lord Jesus Church was on its way to reclaiming its heritage in a way that would give it new vision for ministry.

LESSONS FOR LEADING

Our look at Lord Jesus Church through the lens of sociological concepts points out some of the ways that sociology can be a practical ally for church leaders.

Church as Choice

For one thing, it reminds us—especially in the American political context—of the power of the social group that is formed by voluntary association. To be free to join together for religious purposes provides individuals and communities with many more options than historically have been possible in many parts of the world. That freedom to associate is being exercised in the current generation perhaps more than ever before.[14] Its exercise is like a two-edged sword: persons will join a church if and when they choose, but they also could leave it. When association is voluntary, churches must be more attentive to motivating their members in their commitments to vision and ministry.

Not Too Big for our Britches

For another thing, a sociological interpretation of church places the realities of class and status in bold relief. It seems difficult for many congregations to deal with these factors very objectively. Because class and status are both expressed in, and shaped by, congregations, the very experience of congregations tells us a lot about the function of religion in society. The "rub" comes when class and status as describable features meet the expectations of a congregation's purported theological message. That is, for Christians, "the way things are" is not necessarily "the way things should be." The gospel claim for new life and wholeness contains a dimension that class and status often starkly reveal.

On the one hand, human beings seek, and legitimately need, a certain amount of acceptance and influence. These are desires that have to be met in a social arena, and congregations provide one such arena. On the other hand, what happens—or has happened— to a congregation that becomes known as the church to join in order to be considered for membership in the local country club? When do the workings of economic position and community influence deter—or worse, hamper—the congregation's calling to follow the gospel? As Christians, as biblical people, we must admit that the human realities lifted up by these sociological categories do indeed sometimes find themselves in tension with the normative claims of the gospel.

Characteristics to Assess

Class and status can be utilized by a congregation to check on the parameters that it has developed for its overarching characteristics. Church leaders would raise searching, significant issues by considering the following.

Physical plant and location. Congregations with substantial financial resources and influence in their community can purchase property in the more desirable parts of town that would be populated or frequented by persons most "like them"; they will also construct buildings as attractive as they can afford, furnishing them with features that appeal to their class and status. By contrast, working-class minority congregations often must take whatever property might be available and affordable, perhaps an abandoned store or dilapidated church building in a much less desirable part of town.

What does your facility's location and current condition suggest about how your congregation is regarded in your community? How well does this social position express your church's understanding of the gospel?

Relationship to the community. Armed with demographic information about a community and its particular congregations, a skilled researcher could predict with some accuracy which churches were highly regarded and which ones were invisible to the public eye. Does this church draw community "movers and shakers" or mostly minimum-wage laborers into its membership? Answering these questions provides a mirror to the dynamics of the area's social and cultural scene.

Which elements of your community's social structure does your congregation attract? Why? How would someone from a different "social location" feel about Christian faith after participating in your Sunday morning worship?

Self-understanding. The realities of class and status tend to act like water in a fishbowl: the fish don't even think about the water, but they know that it is there and that they depend upon it for the way that things happen. The old jokes about Presbyterians being Methodists who got educated, and Episcopalians being Presbyterians who got rich, play off the forces of class and status, even when recognized only implicitly. Once a church tradition moves from working class to middle class, there is a strong pull for the realities of its class and status to wield more influence on the church than do the ideals of its theological tradition.

What are the attitudes that dominate in your congregation about its own self-image? How much of that image is influenced clearly by theological views? And how clearly are its self-image and theology tied together?

Definition of mission activity. Churches in lower classes tend to view mission in clearly defined evangelistic terms, that is, that individuals must be confronted with the decision to be saved. Their worship, education, and fellowship activities are inclined to undergird this "soul-saving" mission and hence prepare members to engage in it. Implicitly, the lower-class church sees itself reaching out primarily to its socioeconomic peers, to help them gain the surer footing that they themselves believe they have gained. Middle-class churches tend to engage in a combination of financial offerings and a few hands-on mission projects that would be seen by their community as culturally acceptable. For many of these congregations, the offerings are annual funds in which they participate with their denomination. The choice of direct-involvement projects is fairly predictable: food pantries, holiday volunteering at a homeless shelter, teen mission trips to a different region of the country, toy and coat drives, and so on. These reflect an implicit belief of the middle class that people who are "down and out" need some help, so that they can apply themselves again and get back on their own two feet.

Upper-middle class churches often reflect an ambiguity of mission definition. On the one hand, they usually are active through significant financial giving, at a level that keeps denominational officials attentive. On the other hand, a certain degree of class insularity leads such congregations to keep their direct contact with persons and situations of long-term basic need quite limited. Such congregations might establish foundations that provide funds generously to projects of their choosing, such as educational advancement and innovative ministry projects that someone else is doing.

In what ways does your congregation engage in mission? How does this activity reflect its theology? its class and status? Where do you see points of tension?

Not Too "This," Not Too "That"

Besides highlighting the realities of choice and class status, a third way that sociology can help church leaders is through the concepts of movement and institution. Local churches could seek to create a productive tension between the extremes of new vitality and established patterns. Newer churches would realize that they cannot survive on the strength of personalities and close relationships alone; some structures and processes will need to be developed. Older churches will have the opposite challenge—to create some movementlike activity in their congregation that will not be stifled by old structures and habits.

Researchers Hadaway and Roozen argue in a similar way for the renewal of mainstream Protestant denominations.[15] Speaking as sociological scholars of the American religious scene, they point out something that is so obvious as to be overlooked: denominations grow as individuals join local churches. They propose that efforts to revitalize local churches must be undertaken more as a movement and less like an institution. For instance, if a denominational agency wants genuine and influential renewal in its midst, it should not appoint a committee to oversee it! It should rather encourage a network of leaders who feel drawn to promote renewal.[16] This network can benefit as a movement from charismatic leadership, thus being constrained by only a minimum of institutional trappings.

One of the practical problems facing congregations who say they want to "grow" is that of perspective. A church that has existed for many decades probably does not have any members alive who can remember what the "movement"-phase days were like. In these churches, the best that the collective memory can do is to recall "glory days," when a new and grander facility was constructed, when there were lots of people of all ages and many activities of a social, spiritual, and benevolent nature. Longtime members in such well-established churches have at best a dim awareness of what movementlike faith looks and feels like. All of the vitality and determination that made it possible for the "glory days" to emerge becomes codified—and, in effect, trivialized—through creating the church's official history.

Some congregations in recent years have attempted to address in part the challenge of staying movementlike by hiring an associate pastor for membership development and assimilation. This strategy holds both promise and peril for the institutionalized congregation. Its promise lays in its effort to intentionally draw new members into a strong, positive relationship with the congregation. People who volunteer to be part of a social group need to become invested in that group—or they eventually will volunteer not to participate! The peril in this staffing pattern lies in the temptation of the stagnant institutionalized church to suppose that all it needs to do is just add another program. That would be an institutional solution for what both history and sociology tell us is more complex.

Instead, there needs to be something movement-like in the way that persons move through the complex-but-subtle rite of passage from first-time church visitor to active church member. The kind of "ministry team" style that Bill Easum promotes[17] would help to keep the visitor-to-active member challenge as energetic and flexible as possible. Easum's model implicitly calls for radically reducing the institutional elements of our congregations, in favor of movement-like processes.

One way that denominational trends seem to be reflecting some awareness of the concept of movement is in the way that job descriptions are designed for pastors of new church starts. Here it is clear that the particular tasks and the kind of personality that would enjoy these tasks are quite distinct, when the challenge is to begin a congregation from scratch. To some extent, the founding pastor has to have some Weberian charisma, a certain appeal and magnetism. Churches in traditions with little connectional structure tend to depend upon this characteristic; their risk, however, is that the church focuses upon the pastor's personality and style too much. In the latter case, churches often founder seriously when its first pastor leaves the scene. Regardless of the inherent problems surrounding new church leadership, the one factor that has to be considered is to what extent membership in the new church is perceived as voluntary. For the most part, American society promotes choice in religion. New churches have to make an appealing case for themselves, being surrounded as they are by many other church choices, some of which are well-established.

Church Along the Edges

A fourth and final suggestion in this chapter for engaging sociology as a tool for church leadership comes from the discussion of the concept of marginality. Although often used in public discourse in the narrow sense of being dispossessed and disenfranchised, marginality also can be applied more broadly and, in a sense, more neutrally. When an African American congregation considers the biblical story of the Exodus, it identifies its own history and experience of oppression with that of the Israelites in Egypt. This correlation of marginality is both sociologically and theologically sound and should never be dismissed. At the same time, however, persons and communities with privilege and opportunity also can use marginality to reframe some aspect of their own experience as well. Facing the reality of "being different" in some respect can generate powerful insights for Christians and churches, as they seek to be authentic and earnest in doing gospel ministry.

Following the example of Lord Jesus Church in Fieldtown, one way that a congregation can engage marginality is through its own heritage. Perhaps there are stories, even painful ones, in your congregation's past that can be brought to light and framed in a new way. Churches that are "just like everyone else" are likely to be churches that do little to live out the gospel. Churches that understand how they "are different" can draw strength from that difference for fresh vision and work in the name of Christ.

CONCLUSION

In a society that prizes individuality, the life of Christian congregations has been hampered by the "cocoon syndrome." We have tended to treat our relationship with a congregation as one that is defined by a hodgepodge of individuals, each one carrying his or her own small, private world of religion—cocoons—in which each seeks to keep comfortable. Our churches have tended to be viewed as "filling stations" where people "pull in," like a motor vehicle, to get "gassed up" (and occasionally tuned up) for the next week. What happens when the individuals of a congregation get together or work together becomes implicitly understood as a function of primarily meeting their personal needs.

It is not the intent of this chapter or book to argue that the needs of individuals are not important, either to the church or to God! After all, as Jesus implies in his most famous sermon (Matt. 6:25–34), God is intimately involved with this creation! Yet the creation includes more than us humans, and we humans are more than the aggregate of our private experiences. We exist, biologically and socially, in community. Further, the Christian faith that emerged two millennia ago depended upon community for its expression.

Concepts from sociology can be used in churches for two beneficial purposes. One is to analyze and interpret the realities of congregational existence more comprehensively and effectively. I hope that the reader is beginning to get a feel for how this kind of analysis can be done by those who directly serve congregations. The second purpose is for planning and action. A church's vision, the various programming that flows from the vision, the constituents who are served by that programming, and the processes for making things function well—all four of these parts of a congregation's life will be powerfully shaped when we move beyond the cocoon syndrome. In this view, our life as "the people of God" and "the body of Christ" pulses with vigor and results.

THREE

MAKING YOUR WAY AROUND THE VILLAGE

Congregation as Bearer of Meaning

He was one frustrated young pastor. Had he not thought carefully about the need that he was trying to help the church address? Did he not "go through all the proper channels" in order to institute the idea properly? Were not the committee members genuinely persuaded by his clearly laid out reasons for proposing the idea? He even pointed out theological warrants that emphasized the church as a body of active laypeople. And, when the committee brought their recommendation to the church board, had not the board voted unanimously to approve the project?

Then why was nothing happening? Why were the elected leaders of the congregation doing nothing to implement what they had formally agreed to do? What had their pastor, in his second year with them, failed to do to make things happen? Had his theology of ministry fallen on deaf ears? What had he yet to learn about this people?

A story like this one rings with authenticity for many a pastor and church leader! Conscientious pastors, even those who "believe in the system," often discover that the system does not always work as one expects it to. There is more to "the system" than meets the eye! In the language of modern business, church leaders come to realize that their congregations are more than organizational bureaucracies. Sometimes, what a pastor or lay leader might have learned in a management course turns out not to adapt well when it is used with a congregation. Why is this the case?

The answer to this question is not likely to be clear yet. In chapter one, we saw how the broad discipline of sociology can help church leaders to look at the congregation from a different, much wider, point of view. Even though Americans live in a society that prizes individualism, the reality is that human experience always carries the influence of community. Churches, like many other organizations today, are social groups. Any kind of social group will develop characteristics that cannot be reduced simply to those of the persons who comprise the group. Hence, churches also are communities that take on an identity of their own; to understand a church adequately requires the ability to view it in social terms.

Yet, as we know, not every social group is the same. Neither is every church. When I was growing up in a small town in Oregon, my contact with social groups was fairly limited. It included my family, the small church we attended, the public school system with just three grade schools, one junior high school, and one high school, and the local businesses. What opened me to the wider world, even more than television, was *National Geographic Magazine*. As soon as I could read, I remember becoming absorbed in the photographs and maps of every issue. It was not only the geography itself that captivated me; it was also in slowly realizing that other communities of people in faraway places lived very differently than my friends and I. The ones who fascinated me the most were those who lived in simple villages, with virtually everything they owned and used made by hand.

Later, in college, I took a cultural anthropology course and learned more about the ways of these kinds of peoples. It felt strange to try to understand the logic and view of the world that permeated these communities. These people did not know that the earth revolves around the sun or that certain bacteria cause certain kinds of infections. Yet, when one reads researchers like Margaret Mead, one is drawn tantalizingly inside the life of these peoples whose life is so different. We are confronted with the challenge of trying to empathize, to understand what it is like to live as they do. Scientific truth aside, one significant issue discussed in our college class was whether modern Western societies could claim to be superior because they had "improved on" so much.

The tools of cultural anthropology do not have to be limited to studying communities that are "primitive" and "non-Western." As a broad concept, culture is certainly recognized as part of every human community. However, I think that we Westerners must admit to a bias against wanting to use labels that often imply, even inadvertently, inferiority. I am claiming that this bias works to our disadvantage. We could learn much more about ourselves by taking many of the same concepts that cultural anthropologists have developed for their "primitive" studies and applying them in modern Western life.

In recent years, a growing number of Christian scholars and practitioners have begun to do just this. James Hopewell utilized the cultural elements of his training in comparative religion to speak of studying congregations in anthropological terms.[1] Others have followed suit[2] or made the same point in their own ways.[3] Yet perhaps the more significant work in applying cultural anthropology to modern life has come from researchers in organizational studies. We will see more about certain aspects of their work in the final chapter.

This chapter introduces you to the image of the congregation as a village. It takes a number of recognized concepts from cultural anthropology and suggests ways in which these concepts help to explain the complex phenomena that we call "congregation." By the end of this chapter, the reader should begin to get a feel for viewing the congregation as something like one of those villages pictured in *National Geographic,* which opened my world as a child. A "village" perspective can help the young pastor at the beginning of the chapter understand why his "reasonable" strategy fell short. Let us begin, then, with some very broad notions and work our way toward some more specific ones.

THE CONCEPT OF "CULTURE": DEFINITIONS

As a formal scholarly discipline, cultural anthropology began to emerge around the turn of the twentieth century. Researchers, many from large universities in Europe and the United States, traveled to non-Western continents to do field study of many peoples who lived as their ancestors had for untold centuries. Others also began to study native peoples who still lived on ancient lands being taken over by Western industrialization.

As they observed and gathered data on the peoples' daily life, habits, dwellings, special events, and customs, early cultural anthropologists began to create their own language. This new terminology expressed the new concepts that the researchers developed to explain what they saw. Some of the more influential of these researchers include the likes of Bronislaw Malinowski, Margaret Mead, Victor Turner, and Clifford Geertz.

How do anthropologists define culture? Their wording and emphases might vary some among them, but most of these definitions include notions of collective human action that reveals some kind of order. One textbook on the subject offers two brief and simple definitions; culture is "learned and shared kinds of human behavior (including the material results of this behavior)"[4]; culture can also be described as "the patterned way of life shared by a group of people."[5] A scholar who has applied cultural concepts to the study of modern organizations makes the same point with an emphasis on meaning: "Culture is the system of such publicly and collectively adapted meanings operating for a given group at a given time."[6]

At the level of a village or small town, these definitions of culture operate in a fairly straightforward manner. However, in the much more complex, technologically driven world in which we now live, it seems that our application of the concept of culture itself must become more complex and somewhat nuanced. Thus, as we think about the way that culture functions for most of us, we realize that it does so at more than one level or layer. Here is one way to distinguish these layers.

Macroculture is a term that can be used to describe broad elements of culture in a nation that is large and diverse. The United States of America, for example, cover a continent three thousand miles wide and more than a thousand miles long in most places. In spite of many noted regional differences, there are some basic perceptions, values, and behaviors that characterize life in the U.S.A. Notions of individual freedom, opportunity, social mobility, political participation, and the like have grown out of the American experience. This was the case even before radio, motion pictures, television, and other technologies with which Americans are so familiar emerged as further unifying agents.

Mesoculture describes those elements of culture that live within a macroculture but that characterize a particular region or ethnic group. In Canada, Quebec has a mesoculture based in its French heritage that distinguishes it in some significant ways from the British macroculture of the nation generally. Garrison Keillor's fictional "Lake Wobegon, Minnesota" symbolizes the Scandinavian mesoculture in the upper Midwest, present there through immigration of ethnic groups. By contrast, the independent and "can-do" attitude of the western United States reveals a mesoculture shaped much less by a particular ethnic heritage than by the challenges of history and geography.

Microculture can be used to describe the cultural idiosyncrasies of a much more confined geographic space. This would include a town, a rural county that is not spread out, or a city neighborhood. In some situations, an immigrant ethnic group that lives in a small space would represent a microculture, unless and until—if ever—it populated a significant-sized region of a nation. Microculture helps us understand the kinds of nuances of culture in an otherwise homogeneous area; these nuances develop out of the particular histories, experiences, and personalities that dominate that local population. Neighborhoods in large U.S. cities such as New York and Chicago have had microcultures for generations; with population growth and further immigration, metropolitan areas all around the United States now also bear numerous microcultures. Although on a much smaller scale, so also do many small American towns.

Organizational culture is perhaps the newest way that the concept of culture can be distinguished. As such, it probably is less familiar and at first consideration might seem to be an odd application. Why use culture to explain the behavior of modern organizations? Have they not been established on other kinds of principles—such as rationality, efficiency, and specialization?

Researchers in recent years[7] have been discovering that concepts of culture go a long way in explaining many kinds of behavior in complex organizations, even among those that were designed as "rational-legal bureaucracies." In other words, when an organization is viewed through the lens of culture, it reveals its own version of a "patterned way of life shared by a group of people." Using culture, this argument continues, helps us understand aspects of the organization's existence that have been overlooked or underappreciated. This will be true whether the organization is NASA, Mary Kay Cosmetics, or the Grateful Dead Fan Club.

To illustrate how these four layers of culture actually function, let us consider the experience of an immigrant community in the United States—say, Korean. As Korean individuals and families move to the United States, they establish residences, find employment, shop for necessities and other goods, send their children to school, learn at least the rudiments of a very different language, socialize with each other, and so on. They will maintain many customs and promote many values that "immigrated" with them, even as their children assimilate more readily to the layers of American culture.

Many of the first Korean immigrants of recent years also were interested in maintaining their Christianity, so they founded churches. In those churches we see a fascinating, and often confusing and troubling, mixture of layers of culture. The immigrants left one macroculture that was very familiar to live in another that is in most respects unfamiliar. They are now a microculture, that now must also adapt to the peculiarities of the region in which they now live (mesoculture), as well as to the immediate community (a new microculture). Their church (organizational culture) will blend elements of the old macro- and microcultures with new cultural elements from all levels that now impinge themselves upon them.

One final way of slicing the cultural pie cuts in a different way than these four designations. It is the notion of subculture. A textbook definition of subculture highlights how the pattern of the subculture "plays second fiddle" in its particular setting. For subculture is "a system of perceptions, values, beliefs, and customs that are significantly different from those of the dominant culture."[8] One immediate implication of this notion is that what qualifies as a subculture depends upon the overall context. Compared to its community, for example, most organizational cultures will act as subcultures to the microculture of the community. That microculture often is one of several subcultures in the region's mesoculture, which is in turn a subculture to the macroculture. If this sounds confusing, it certainly can be! If it sounds unnecessarily complicated, that depends on how accurate is the assessment of the setting under consideration, based upon careful observation.

At any rate, the claim is offered: that anthropology's concept and use of culture is rich and nuanced. It can be utilized even for our sophisticated, electronic world that on the surface appears so different from the villages in *National Geographic*. As members of this electronic world, our churches can also benefit from this kind of analysis. Beyond the terms already discussed, there are several others that we will introduce in this chapter.

SOME BASIC CONCEPTS FROM CULTURAL ANTHROPOLOGY

More specifically, these concepts are common to cultural anthropology textbooks and help us to hone in on a number of significant features of congregational life. They are: beliefs, values, and norms; myth and story; ritual and ceremony; space and location; symbol; mana; heroes (and villains); and liminality and communitas. We turn our attention to them now.

Beliefs, Values, and Norms

In a significant way, every culture is an embodiment of a particular set of beliefs, values, and norms. *Beliefs* encompass the worldview that the community has developed to make sense out of its experience, both past and present, of the world that it knows and in which it functions. Historically, beliefs were expressed metaphorically through stories and images. *Values and norms* are standards of behavior that are expected within the group to be taken seriously; violation of these standards often leads to grave consequences, not only for the violator but also for the community. Much of a member's knowledge of the community's beliefs and values comes from informal learning experiences, rather than through explicit training (although we will see later that certain key beliefs and values are usually highly ritualized).

Cross-cultural contact quickly raises the issue of a culture's beliefs and values. There is the story of the Christian missionary who goes to a particular primitive tribe in order to convert them. In his early contact with the tribe, the missionary tries to get oriented. He wants to know about the village, but also about what is beyond their village. Pointing beyond a steep hill some distance away, he asks innocently, "What is over there?"

The village elders look at each other as their eyes widen, and they murmur to each other for a few moments. Finally one of them responds, "Oh, that is a place of great danger. We never go that way."

"Why not?" the missionary persists.

"Because of the fearsome creatures that live there," another elder replies.

Imagining them to be referring to something like a panther or a tiger, the missionary asks again with innocence, "And what are they?"

The elders confer quietly again before one of them turns to the missionary to pronounce with great solemnity, "They are watermelons."

"What?" The missionary's face wrinkles with incomprehension.

"Watermelons," the elder repeats. Seeing no intended mischief in their eyes, the missionary sputters out a reply as if to hear himself think.

"Your village does not go over that hill because watermelons grow over there?"

Looking at him together, the elders nod their heads slowly in agreement with the stunned missionary's statement.

We will return to finish this story later in the chapter. Even what we have heard of it so far helps to point out a couple of insights about the role of beliefs and norms in any community. One is that they are shaped by the particular experiences of that community. A second is that, while the beliefs and values of one's own culture "make sense" to those within it, they do not necessarily make sense to those from outside. Descriptively speaking, then, there are no universal beliefs, since they all are mediated through the particular features of the specific community.

Myth and Story

Closely related to beliefs, values and norms are the ways in which a culture's most fundamental understandings of reality are expressed. *Myth* is a term that does *not* mean "something that is not true." Rather, it refers to accounts of the nature of things that a culture imbues with a holy status and force.[9] How the world came to be, how humans were created and what their relationship to other creatures is, why human existence is the way it is—these and similar questions probe mythic aspects of human perspective.

Myths usually are framed and conveyed by the universal medium of *story*. Stories not only explain sacred and evil forces in a particular culture's world, they also pass on many other kinds of information that the culture deems important. Virtually every known human culture created or creates stories about earlier experiences, about heroes and villians, about why certain aspects of daily life are the way that they are, and so on. Theses stories both preserve and transmit elements of culture. Knowing and understanding the stories of any given culture opens very wide the door to understanding its people.

A compelling presence. In religion, the role of myth and story is woven tightly into its fabric. The creation accounts in Genesis 1 and 2 are religious myth familiar to church people. Stories about other events and persons were also recorded in the Bible because of the important interpretations accorded them in the past by earlier biblical communities. However, myth and story are not confined to religion. Talk to people who have lived in your town or neighborhood for most of their life, and you will be treated to interesting stories, and even a mythical tale or two, about what it was like in "good ol' days." The Western, as literature and as motion picture, is an art form peculiar to the United States, as it spins stories of characters, places, events, and the like based upon many often implicit myths about "the West."

Ritual and Ceremony

Clearly, cultures do more than "talk" about themselves; they also do things. Much behavior in any given culture reveals pattern and order that is aimed at specific purposes of different kinds and varying importance. When this kind of behavior is enacted by an individual, it commonly is known as *ritual*. When such patterned behavior is more complex and involves the community in a public display, it takes on the character of *ceremony*.

In other words, ceremonies tend to be composed of the routines of rituals that are clustered together and acted out, symbolizing particular cultural values. Rituals can be as perfunctory as the way a child brushes her teeth before bed or as sacred as the same child saying her prayers a few minutes later. Similarly, ceremonies can range from the silly to the sublime, depending upon the group's purposes.

It is very apparent that religion involves ritual and ceremony in very significant ways. Many of these behaviors become formalized, in private devotional practices and clearly in liturgies. Yet, especially for ritual, formality is not necessary. In fact, one of the challenges for a cultural outsider is in figuring out what rituals indicate one's being an "insider." Later in this chapter, we will look at ritual and ceremony in churches and see how very potently these concepts describe much of what occurs in churches.

Space/Location

Culture is also influenced by its sense of place and use of space. Where people live, how they adapt and/or fill their residences, what and how they eat, where they gather for public events—these decisions and behaviors are affected by the space that is available to a community and how it chooses to use the space. Until very recently in history, space was highly influenced by the unalterable features of geography and climate. For today's modern world, these two factors have been somewhat subdued by technological abilities: new subdivisions of houses in the United States look pretty much the same, regardless of the region of the country where they are located.

Churches use space, too. For most traditions, the sanctuary represents the central value for church space, because it houses the congregation's worship life. Historically, church structures were dominated by—if not entirely consisted of—space directly related to worship. Again, however, developments in the twentieth century have led to much more diverse use of space and, hence, of facilities. Education, fellowship, meals, administration, counseling, recreation, and other church activities often are given their own space. And the values and rituals associated with each of these spaces will vary, depending on their perceived relationship to the church's purposes.

Symbol

Simply stated, symbols are objects or images that stand for something other than what materially constitutes them. Every culture develops symbols of its own, which—like its myths and stories—do not automatically or readily transfer their meaning into other cultures. Symbolic power rests not in analytical articulation but in a recognized representation of, and compelling appeal to, key aspects of the culture, that is, in its beliefs, values, and myths. The American flag symbolizes a varied, and sometimes diverse, cluster of beliefs, values, and myths associated with the United States.

names symbols unique to your cong

Trophies symbolize skilled achievement in a contest. Wedding bands and rings symbolize a special kind of lifelong partnership. The cross symbolizes Christian faith.

Crosses are, of course, not the only symbols that churches use. Since there are no a priori limits to what can or cannot function as a symbol, any particular church could create its own powerful but idiosyncratic symbols that would mean little to neighboring congregations. Plaques commemorating beloved pastors, communion tables, memorial windows, gardens, pulpits—many objects in a church building that have instrumental or esthetic purpose can also become imbued with some kind of symbolism.

Mana

All of the concepts that we have described so far in this section should be relatively easy for the reader to identify and relate to. In discussing mana, however, we might be venturing into unfamiliar territory. In cultural anthropology, *mana* is a term that describes the power that a community recognizes to be potentially operative in its midst. Many cultures perceive the world as full of forces that must be reckoned with. Mana describes those forces that are available to and in the community, under conditions that the culture comes to designate. While mana can be used for good, it also must be handled carefully, for it characteristically appears in ambiguous circumstances and relationships.[10]

By continuing the missionary and watermelon story, we can see something of the nature of mana. You remember that the missionary has been told by the village elders that the place where the watermelons grow beyond the hill is a place that they avoid. After a few moments of incredulity, the missionary blurts out, "But what can the watermelons possibly do to you?"

This time, as the elders look at each other, their eyebrows rise and furrow as they glance back at the missionary. An elder replies, "Ah, but the watermelons possess great power that can harm our people."

Pausing for a moment to see if the elders are serious, the missionary then turns abruptly and begins to walk toward the hill. "I will show you," he stammers through his march-like footsteps, "that you have nothing to fear from this harmless, delicious fruit." As the elders watch the missionary treading off toward the watermelon patch, they call to him wildly. When they see that he does not slow down, they join the women and children in the huts, who are peering from the open doors at all the activity.

A minute after the missionary disappears over the top of the hill, he reappears in a pose of triumph, holding a large watermelon over his head. "Here is your dreaded enemy!" he shouts. "It is nothing more than a fruit, something to eat. See how easily it is crushed," he brags as he drops the spherical fruit onto the ground in front of him. The village gasps audibly. "And look," the victorious missionary continues, "it tastes wonderful!" He picks up a section of the watermelon, bites a large piece of the red fruit, chews it with a smile and concludes his demonstration with a testimony. "This is delicious! Your children will love it!"

That night, after the missionary goes to bed, the elders meet. Who is this person who has come to help them, yet who has the power to destroy the dreaded watermelons? He must be even more dangerous than the watermelons themselves! So, by consent, the elders agree to what must be done. By morning, the missionary is still in his bed, but he has died.

Our zealous missionary failed in one of the first lessons in cross-cultural understanding. He did not respect the beliefs or understand the mana of this community. Instead, he quickly violated the use of the village's mana, hence paying for the consequences dearly. And the village was even more convinced that their belief about the watermelons was true.

Heroes/Villains

In other words, the missionary completely undermined his chances to become one of that culture's *heroes*. Rather, he entered their folkore as a *villain*, a stranger who flaunted foolishly with the evil powers of the rightfully feared watermelons. As mirror concepts, hero and villain are figures in a culture who represent what the community most cherishes. They personify its fundamental values and norms by symbolizing either their adherence (hero) or violation (villain). As such, heroes in particular undergird the culture: they embody appropriate achievement; they act as role models; they have developed an effective relationship with other cultures.[11]

American heroes of historic stature include presidents like George Washington and Abraham Lincoln. Ethnic heroes who have moved more into the macrocultural level include Martin Luther King Jr. and Willie Mays. Sports heroes abound, but few with the broad appeal in recent years of basketball's Michael Jordan. Business tycoons, philanthropists, soldiers, occasionally religious figures like Mother Teresa, teachers, entertainers, and others all appeal to different American subcultures in different ways. Similarly, people like Jack the Ripper, Jesse James, and Al Capone take on villain status because of the extent to which they flagrantly trespass the boundaries of cultural acceptability. It is also worth pointing out that, when cultural standards change, heroes and villains are more difficult to identify without ambiguity.

Liminality and Communitas

Our final set of concepts from cultural anthropology is drawn from research on what are known as "rites of passage."[12] This theory argues that many cultures develop elaborate processes to usher the transition occasioned by significant life changes (such as birth, puberty, marriage, and death). Transition begins with some way of separating those involved with their usual routines and settings. This separation leads to an experience of being "betwixt and between," that is, of not having the previous status anymore but not yet having arrived at another one. This ambiguity is called *liminality*, and it creates both psychological and sociological effects.

While some modern Westerners might proudly suppose that our macroculture has no equivalent to tribal puberty rites, one need only to consider such phenomena as fraternity initiations to recognize that similar purposes are being served, even in our "sophisticated" society! But the hazing and intimidation of present-day initiations are not the only forms of liminality that we can observe around us. When a natural disaster occurs, the usual forms of sociocultural dynamics are temporarily disrupted. Role importance shifts as emergency measures kick into gear. Those who grieve losses often come from a wide spectrum of the community's socioeconomic constituency. They interact with each other in unusual and sometimes intimate ways that typically disappear once "normalcy" is restored. In more recent years, experts work with victims over a period of time, providing them with support that comes partly in the form of new information that will help them as the immediate effects of the disaster subside.

It is this new set of dynamics, the bonding that occurs during the period of ambiguity, that anthropologists call *communitas*. In many cultures, communitas is planned to occur symbolically during festive occasions. These positive experiences seem to help strengthen the community's capacity for dealing with uncertainty. Because they are safe and controlled, they in a sense rehearse the people in the experience of liminality. Elders pass on new information—through mythical stories, symbols, and norms—that becomes keys for passing into the new status. Communitas thus becomes a shared memory, but also an empowering moment, for those who endure it.

THE CONGREGATION AS A VILLAGE

We have just looked summarily at a number of concepts from cultural anthropology, selected because of their potential to apply in illuminating ways to congregations. That discussion prepares us to speak of congregations in these terms. We now turn to this task, both generally and specifically. Our purpose is to put some useful flesh on the metaphor of the congregation as a village.

Churches as "Irrational"

By way of general impression, I want to argue first why a cultural perspective on congregations helps us to understand what I call a church's inherent prerationality or "irrationality." By this term I do not mean that people in churches don't think! The point is a little more subtle than that. It is rather that congregations do not decide and behave the way that they do primarily on the basis of logical reasoning processes. The key word in this explanation perhaps is "primarily," for certainly people in churches who make decisions and lead activities use their minds. Yet, from an anthropological perspective, reason becomes a tool in the service of other, stronger factors that drive the church as a culture-bearing community. Hopefully, too, those stronger factors include a theological understanding of the gospel, which Paul called "foolishness to the Gentiles" (see 1 Cor. 1:22–25).

Let's see if a story can illustrate this claim. A denominational executive was working with two urban churches whose neighborhoods had experienced significant changes since the congregations were first established several decades ago. Both churches were concerned about their own futures: membership and attendance were dropping, members were aging and moving farther away, financial resources were declining. At the executive's suggestion, the boards of these two churches agreed to participate for a year together on the question of merging with each other. A six-member merger task force was appointed from both congregations.

Over a period of several months, this task force studied a lot of hard data: demographic summaries of census information about their respective neighborhoods (population, ethnic mix, education, income levels, home values, etc.), as well as cost-effectiveness analyses of the two physical facilities. They were given estimates of how much money it would take to: a) continue as they were, without merging, keeping their own facilities and hiring their own pastors; b) merging, selling building A and using building B; c) merging, selling building B and using building A; or d) merging, selling both buildings and relocating to a new or another facility.

During the process, task force members acknowledged the financial benefits of merging. The big question in their minds centered on facilities; which of the other three options would they be willing to pursue? After much discussion, a meeting was scheduled for a vote. How do you suppose the vote turned out?

On the night of the vote, every task force member from church A voted to sell church B and keep church A, while every task force member from church B voted to sell church A and keep church B! From that point, there was no further progress; the merger conversations had come to a halt.

Later, the executive acknowledged privately that the process used in the merger conversation did not help the task force members make a helpful decision. He had expected that these active, concerned church members would realize the "nuts-and-bolts" parameters of their respective situations and agree to a merger model that would benefit them both. Yet other forces were at work within the members, forces of memory, loyalty, and pride. These forces do not readily bow to the "power" of reason, which often is represented by the bottom line of a financial ledger. These forces are the kind that we have sought to identify in this chapter with concepts of culture.

To speak of congregations as prerational or "irrational" is not, however, to be seen as negative or derogatory. If culture is indeed the warp and woof of a community, its features emerge and take shape over a period of years, as the community exists and experiences many things. Culture cannot be changed overnight, especially if you assume that the members of that culture have a say in the matter. In other words, as we saw in chapter 1, congregations in our era increasingly have taken on characteristics of what sociologists term "voluntary associations." The culture of a voluntary association is deeply shaped by the basic belief that, because the organization has a choice about existing (i.e., it is not mandated by a government or state), the organization and its members guide what it will be and do. (This concept, "voluntary association," will be discussed again in chapter 4.) Such an orientation does not become automatically or rigidly subjected simply to the results of "logical" discourse.

East Park neighborhood[13] witnessed a successful church merger because of the key role that one pastor gave to the "prerational" or "irrational" element of congregational life. Both the Methodist and the Presbyterian churches in East Park had lost many members in recent years, and the congregation was aging. All the demographic information that the city's urban renewal department provided indicated that the two congregations would not long survive on their own. Since the Rev. Tod Maclean was serving both churches, he was able to assess the situation and set a course of pastoral action toward merger. For this course, Tod had gathered information from and consulted with, not only the city, but also books on church renewal and the appropriate denominational staff.

Tod's strategy, however, did not begin with—or even focus upon—a "rational" solution. Instead, Tod centered his pastoral activity upon the two congregations' memberships. On the one hand, he paid many pastoral calls, during which the future of the respective churches was part of the conversation. He worked hard at listening to the concerns that the members expressed, mostly anticipating the loss of a place with so many significant life memories. Tod explained to members about what he was finding out about the neighborhood and the city's plans to purchase old buildings. He did not try to talk them into "his" plan to save both churches. In his sermons for both churches, Tod emphasized the importance of looking ahead and of trusting God.

A point arrived when the churches had only so much time to decide about selling property to the city. By this time, Tod had visited many members' homes. The two congregations appointed a joint committee to explore merger, taking several months to deal with questions of property, finances, endowments, denominational ties, and the like. When the decision to merge was made, a detailed plan was then drawn up and discussed thoroughly among both memberships. Some members suggested changes that the joint committee included in the plan. When the vote on the plan was held, it passed in both congregations by a wide margin.

Pastor Tod had laid the groundwork for a painful and complicated process by visiting, listening, keeping the process open and direct, and creating in worship a spirit of faith and hope. Because he had honored and worked with the cultural, "irrational" foundation of the two congregations, Tod had led them into a merger with which they could live and from which they could willingly benefit.

Since congregational culture is prerational or irrational, it is complicated by the complexity of cultural layers, especially on the North American scene. The effects of the 1960s cultural revolution illustrates this point well. Older church members often interpreted social and political protest at the macrocultural level as a difference between the generations. "It's those young people and their ideas," was a sentiment that I myself have heard a number of times from various churches. And to some degree, this is true.[14] Yet, at the same time, the homogeneous perception of the public arena—so clearly epitomized by traditional small-town America—was indeed broken in the 1960s. Consequently, other levels of culture that had not been given much prior voice now made their way to the doors of the churches. It was very difficult for most mainstream Protestant congregations to adjust their culture to that kind of onslaught.

Culture is prerational or irrational, and since churches create, possess, and transmit culture, they also are irrational. But that is not bad or wrong in itself.

Subcultures in Congregations

One of my aims in this chapter is to point out how subtlely complex the phenomenon of a congregation truly is. The concept of subculture assists us in understanding this subtle complexity, for it gives us a tool by which to identify a basic way that this complexity occurs. Persons who a part of a church community—whether adult members, baptized children, unbaptized children of adult members, confirmed youth, regular visitors, or other nonmembers who participate in various church programs and activities—share across a spectrum of cultural elements. The most common is regular corporate worship. In most Christian traditions, worship functions as the central unifying symbol of the church's life; it is what the congregation shares most in common and thus stands for its overall culture.

At the same time, however, within the congregation's life other programs over time can take on something of a life of their own. These could include a choir or choirs, particular fellowship and social organizations, a Sunday school class that has met together for twenty years, a youth group, boards, committees, and the like. With its specific focus and history, a group like this can develop to a point that some of its own beliefs, values, rituals, stories, and so on are somewhat distinguishable from the church's overall culture. Here, then, emerges a subculture within the congregation.

In congregations that are fairly young in years, subcultures are not as evident or influential upon the church's life. As time goes by, however, they do emerge, often on lines of age bracket, class, and gender. By the time that a church has entered, say, its third generation (after about fifty years), subcultures are indeed evident: the women's society, so prevalent and strong in many churches until the 1960s; the Christian Education committee that has been run by the same two persons for twenty-five years; the music program; the loose confederation of adults who try to minister to young people; and so on. In each one of these types of subcultures, it is possible—and likely—that they sometimes will be at odds with the church's general culture. Furthermore, in a congregation that is well-established and past its prime, one of these subcultures tends to dominate the church's agenda.

Notice that the language here highlights culture rather than individual persons. This is perhaps a subtle distinction, but it is most useful—especially in light of one of the points from chapter 1. There we lifted up the fascinating but also confusing issue of concepts of the relationship between self and society, of individual and group. Culture is created out of corporate human existence, in which individuals live. No human being escapes the influence of culture, for socialization involves a process of enculturation. Persons *bear and transmit* culture, but it is because they have participated in some way *in* culture.

So, because culture is social, it exists without depending on any particular persons. If, under some unusual set of circumstances, all the members of a well-established church took the same charter tour of the Holy Land, and if on the return flight home the jet crashed and all the church members died, in a sense the church's culture would not die with them. It would be available in ways to others who wished to enter it and participate in it. Why? because a church building full of memories, equipment, rooms, symbols, books, documents, and more, would still be there. While such an incorporation into this "haunted" culture would be only partial, it nonetheless would be possible to some significant degree.

This is a long way of explaining, for one thing, why subcultures in congregations are not wholly "contained" within a few key people. Culture grows out of community and passes throughout it. When decisions must be made and actions undertaken, any contests that arise in the process are not simply between two individuals or two groups in the church; the contest points to a rub between subcultures. In recent American history, church contests have been identified often as differences between the generations. Here we are claiming, however, that it is not merely that the steelworker and the hippie did not see eye to eye. They stood for beliefs, values, behaviors, uses of space, and symbols that were at odds.

Leaders from Cambridge Flats Church spent a day reflecting on their heritage, their town and their beliefs, as they drew together a new vision statement. One of the elements of that statement was a conviction that leaders wanted the church to be intergenerational, that is, to mix older members with children and youth. Over the years, Cambridge Flats Church had functioned in a typical Protestant way, with educational and fellowship activities for separate age groupings. Much smaller now, Cambridge Flats still had strong promise, so the leaders lifted up "all ages" as one of the stars in its vision.

The question was, how to make this part of the vision begin to come to pass? Leaders in Cambridge Flats Church knew that old-time members tended to associate primarily with other members their age; the leaders were also aware that children and youth do not readily warm up to efforts by church adults to include them. So, on their first opportunity, they planned a program designed for all ages. The Advent Festival series included activities in which persons of all ages could participate. Festival planners took care to prepare interesting projects for the congregation to use throughout December and Epiphany. Messages welcoming members to the Festival went out in the church newsletter and in weekly bulletins.

Attendance at the program was less than hoped, even though everyone who did participate enjoyed it. Festival planners realized that virtually none of the old-timers who they had hoped to see did attend. Also, several families who might have been there did not show. The leaders of Cambridge Flats Church were still committed to the intergenerational part of their new vision. Now they realized that traditional planning efforts would not in themselves begin to address the inertia of their congregation's culture. In this case, that inertia was based in cross-generational attitudes that most likely would take time and careful planning to change successfully.

Of course, congregational subcultures are not at all limited to generational ones. Subcultures also develop around programmatic church areas, such as music, women's associations, the board of trustees, longtime staff, etc. The recognition of all such subcultures also helps us to understand what happens when a congregation faces change. During the 1960s, for instance, many macrocultural elements that had dominated for decades (e.g., segregation, standards for sex, marriage, attire, and public discourse) were challenged and significantly modified. Many, if not most, of these changes were considered by longtime members of well-established churches as questionable. But when the macroculture changes, what happens to the organizational culture of the congregation? If there are no subcultures in that congregation with elements that are sympathetic to the macro-changes, the congregation will not respond. No contests will emerge in the congregation's own public arena, and the perceived threat that accompanies change will not appear. As a consequence, the congregation could lose an opportunity to adjust its Christian witness in a way that would speak freshly to new situations.

Mana in the Congregation

Change in a culture can occur only when mana is appropriated and used effectively. Congregations that have existed enough years to have charter members or longtime members live with an implicit understanding of what mana is available, and to whom. Think about the persons in your congregation who truly have "the power to make things happen." They are not necessarily those in elected positions of authority; they likely have been members for more than ten years; they are persons whose opinion is well-considered by other members.

A congregation does not "decide" who receives which mana and who does not; this kind of endowment happens in subtle ways that can be only partially explained. Church members do not get together once a year and dole out mana as though it were rations or prizes. Rather, throughout the lived experiences of a church, as its values are tested in concrete situations, the members observe how each other behaves. Those who are perceived to support the church's mission and life gain the kind of familiarity, trust, and respect that gives rise to church influence. Typically, a handful of members are (at least implicitly) recognized as possessing greater influence than others. This influence becomes power, in both small and major ways, within the congregation's life. Whether beneficent or self-serving, the congregation's dynamics of mana shape much of its existence.

Notice also in this general description that pastors are not mentioned. That omission is deliberate on my part, for a good reason. Pastors do not automatically possess much mana. Certainly they fill a role as pastor, one usually of some high congregational regard. However, the concept of mana serves in part to remind us that "office" and "influence" are not the same thing. Many pastors fail to grasp this significant distinction; their failure not only frustrates them, it hurts the church that they serve.

Think for a moment, by way of example, of a church you know that receives its pastors by appointment. In an episcopal tradition (see chapter 6), a bishop or similar official exercises the final authority on which pastor serves which parish. Pastoral tenures in these denominations tend to be noticeably shorter than in churches that call the pastor themselves. What effect does this difference have on mana? It suggests the congregation's power will tend to reside in the congregation, especially among a few of the older, longtime, active members. For such congregations, pastors come and go; it is thus more challenging to develop deep, trusting relationships with them. Consequently, those who come to exercise pivotal influence in that congregation tend to be those who have been active and trustworthy for a long time—that is, members. Sometimes these persons hold major congregational offices; sometimes—as is often the case with a "church mother" in an African American congregation—she just knows everybody and everything!

So, to new pastors or church staff members who think that they can do what they want because they work for the church: Beware! The mana might get you!

Every congregation has persons who can exercise mana over certain parts of the congregation's life. Men in the church—even the husbands!—are often powerless against the wishes of the women's group for matters related to the church's kitchen and parlor. But mana is usually much less definable than kitchen rights. New pastors and new church members do well to observe and ask questions, in order to discern the congregation's mana and who has been "granted" what mana for what purposes.

The Congregation's Location and Space

Speaking of church kitchens and parlors also illustrates various ways in which congregations value space. Most church members will agree that its church's primary important space is its sanctuary. "Going to church" almost universally means attending worship in the sanctuary, not attending church school, a social function, or other church program. A sanctuary not only symbolizes what makes churches what they are; but for Christians, worship itself normatively defines a church's self-understanding. Thus, everything that is found in a sanctuary space both shapes and stands for the particular congregation's culture.

This cultural symbolism also includes a congregation's understanding of its position in its community. As we saw in chapter 1, the realities of a church's life are deeply affected by sociological matters such as economic class and social status. Sanctuaries that resemble European cathedrals—high ceilings, carved stone, raised pulpits, elaborate stained-glass windows, and so forth—are much more likely to be constructed in the center of what is at the time the "nicest" part of town. These congregations include a significant constituency that is well-educated, with well-paying jobs, attractive homes in desirable locations, and otherwise influential in the social, business, and governmental affairs of the community. Similarly, sanctuaries that are smaller, modest, and sparse in furnishings, with more emphasis on function than esthetic taste tend to be built where land is available cheaply. Such congregations have fewer financial resources and less status in their communities.

Within the church's other physical facilities, other spaces will be valued and utilized not merely for their defined instrumental function. We have mentioned the church kitchen and the parlor as examples. In many churches, the kitchen traditionally has been one place where the power of women could be safely exercised. Women were in charge of church meals and of anything done in, or used from, the kitchen. The same was true (and often continues to be so!) for the parlor. Interior photographs of churches built by middle-class congregations before 1900 bear evidence of a room handsomely decorated and set apart for functions approved of by the Ladies' Society. In a more contemporary vein, youth groups sometimes "take over" an unused room in a church building. With some trepidation by the board, they will paint it with bright colors and unusual murals, furnishing it with beanbag chairs and donated carpeting, chairs, and sofas.

In these and all other spaces within the church's facilities, it is also the case that members of the various subcultures will value and treat each space somewhat differently. The fellowship hall to children and youth is a great place to play; for retired members, it holds memories of congregational meetings and cherished seasonal events. Contests over use of space in a congregation's physical plant implicitly become contests between different subcultural values. More is at stake than matters of income, efficiency, or the like; it is about what the activity will symbolize about what is important to the congregation.

Space and location is also a feature of the congregation into which the relationships between theology and culture are often deeply enmeshed and difficult to clarify. Consider the following illustration. In at least two Protestant churches in which I have worshipped, there was a fixed, wooden table structure flush to the front wall, and there was also a portable wooden table at the bottom of the chancel steps. In one of the sanctuaries, the fixed table up front was called the "altar" and the other was called the "communion table." For those acquainted with liturgical theology, this arrangement is nonsensical. Either the sanctuary has an altar, which—until the sixteenth century—was the place in all European churches where the sacrifice of Christ is reenacted, or it has—in most Protestant traditions—a "Lord's table," where Jesus' Last Supper with his twelve is commemorated. Neither theology of the Eucharist makes room for two tables. So, in these church buildings, why were they both there?

In this one case, it was due to a compromise that valued accommodation more than doctrine. During its century-plus history, one of the congregations had experienced three different mergers. At the time that its present building was constructed, there were members from Presbyterian, Methodist, Baptist, and Episcopal backgrounds. When the sanctuary was designed and built, one of the more influential members had grown up in the Episcopal church and wanted an altar in the chancel area. In the apparent absence of a theological argument to the contrary, she got her wish. But the Baptists and Presbyterians prevailed when it came to the sanctuary furnishing that was actually used for the sacrament!

In the other sanctuary with two tables, no one seemed to have any idea why they both were there! So much for the power of theology to prevail over the creation of the congregation's idiosyncratic culture.

Belief, Myth, Hero/Villain

When speaking of culture, it is almost impossible to distinguish the various elements as completely separate from one another. As we have spoken in this section about the various concepts, we touch on others as we deal with any one in particular. This is very much the case when dealing with belief, myth, and the hero/villain concept. For the phenomena in a culture that give rise to these particular concepts are densely clustered. Furthermore, as we have just seen, what qualifies in any particular congregation as its beliefs, myths, and heroes/villains is not necessarily dictated by that congregation's ecclesiastical and theological traditions. This "drift" is especially true the more that the congregation has assimilated to a regional mesoculture different from its religious tradition—not to mention macrocultural assimilation.

In other words, when we deal with the beliefs of a congregation's culture, we do not meet a theology that stands alone, as though it has no concrete reference point. Rather, the challenge for most, if not all, congregations is in maintaining a genuine dialogue at all between theology and the culture that emerges. I consulted once with a church where one of the longer-time members candidly told me, "This church was the one that new residents in town found out that, if they joined here, they could get into the country club." The belief that dominated in this case was that the community status of their church was great enough to open doors for privileged opportunities.

Beliefs and norms in a congregation's culture also include standards of *behavior*, many of which go unwritten. In another church, the young and fairly new choir director criticized in a letter to the church board the pastor's behavior during choir rehearsals. Although the tone of the letter was not vindictive nor the account excessive, reaction from the church board overwhelmingly favored the pastor. He had served the church for eight years, during which time the church's membership had grown 20 percent. Two or three of the pastor's strongest social friends within the congregation were active choir members. After a few days of intense telephone activity, the choir director tendered her resignation. She had violated an unwritten belief (pastors are respected) and norm (you don't criticize a pastor in public). Her continued effectiveness as choir director for that church had been lost.

Throughout a congregation's life, it creates and passes on stories of what the members consider important features of their self-understanding. Those stories that continue as part of the collective memories tend to be salutary; they tend to make the congregation look good, whether through a landmark achievement or a struggle that ended in triumph. In reality, however, many of these stories describe events that were more complex and ambivalent. It is when "the whole story" gets lost and cannot be told that a congregation risks losing its ability to maintain a strong culture.

Untold Stories. For a pastor or newer church leader to uncover such "whole stories" takes patience, perseverance, and courage. Consider, by way of dramatic but instructive example, the following phenomenon. Some of the most disturbing news coming from congregations in recent years concerns revelations of sexual abuse by pastors. Since its inception, the Christian faith has represented an ideal of community that values and protects all persons. Now that secret abuse and cover-ups are being exposed, in virtually every denomination across North America, the Church looks less pure and pristine than ever. These new stories—"new" because they are now open to the light of day—are significant for at least two reasons. One reason, as already suggested, is that they paint a picture of Church that is not all flattering. Most of us recoil in deep dismay when we consider the betrayal of trust and safety that these mounting pastoral abuse cases represent. Children and women have been violated, physically, psychologically, and spiritually. There is no way to trivialize the seriousness of such actions by those entrusted with a gospel calling. The Church loses face in the eyes of the world.

This last statement points to a second significant reason why all of a congregation's stories need to be remembered, in spite of their shadow sides. It is because they affect the entire congregation, regardless of how many persons were involved. As we explored in chapter 2, congregations are social groups. Their identity and constitution certainly involves the presence and participation of individual persons, but the congregation itself is more than the sum of its parts. Pastoral abuse is not only something that occurred between the pastor and the other person: because of the roles represented by both parties, pastoral abuse always occurs upon the congregation's stage. This is why judicial actions are appropriate in both ecclesiastical and criminal courts.

My point in referring to pastoral abuse, however, is not to enter the complex theological, pastoral, and legal debates concerning this devastating phenomenon. It is, rather, to emphasize how such a prominent matter illustrates the centrality of myth and story in congregational life. Our Old Testament ancestors were far ahead of us on this matter. In many of the oldest texts, our spiritual forebears' ability to present characters and families in an "unedited" fashion should startle us even today. This one factor alone sets off the Hebrew Scriptures from many others.

Perhaps the quintessential example in this regard is King David, as portrayed in 1 and 2 Samuel. His is a story inextricably interwoven with abuse of both sexual and political power. Not only was Uriah's household violated twice, but Israel's precious, long-awaited kingdom (read here, "the congregation") eventually suffered as a result of David's double-edged lust. In Samuel, the stories about David are not utilized to construct a monolithically favorable myth of the boy-king. Furthermore, it can be argued that it is precisely due to the brutal honesty of this account that the Israelite tradition of faith in Yahweh maintains a realistic strength. Congregations who can embrace this same kind of ambiguity in their own narrative corpus are in a much stronger position to do ministry.

As the David story also readily demonstrates, stories in a congregation can also be about villains, or at least those who would qualify as somewhat less than virtuous. These stories tend not to be written down but are heard privately from sources that go back years. There are stories in congregations about the choir director who divorced his wife and married the choir's favorite soprano, who divorced her husband. In another case, the associate pastor and his wife divorced and the wife later married the pastor, twenty-five years her senior; the associate pastor married that same church's organist. These are stories of which a congregation is not proud, because behavioral norms get violated—or at least pressed to the limit.

Other stories in congregations can villain-ize someone by telling only part of what happened. These stories often develop around staff persons who become scapegoats for implicit contests over the congregation's values and practices. One church that was growing again after a period of membership leveling added a young, new staff pastor to lead youth ministry. He stayed less than three years and by the time he left, so the story goes, was running a home computer business out of his church office. The church leadership after a couple more years decided to try it again, so they expanded the position, gave it a different name, and advertised it as a "new position." It was only after the new staff pastor began working that he became aware of this recent history and how it might affect his own work there.

Congregations tend not to tell questionable stories about themselves. They tend to want to "put their best foot forward" in what others see about them. However, in the long run, churches suffer by hiding from themselves. It is in embracing what looks both good *and* bad in its beliefs, myths, stories, and heroes/villains that a congregation is in a position to keep its culture strong.

Seaview Church leaders came to face this problem of "hero/villain" during a renewal training event. In a discussion of their congregation's history, leaders began to piece together a larger picture of a story revolving around one of their earlier pastors. During this pastor's tenure, several divorces and remarriages within the congregation occurred. The pastor subsequently resigned from the church but remained in town, finding secular employment. Many of the members at the time had liked this pastor very much, but the events of divorce and remarriage that were tied to his tenure left a pall over the congregation. Members never spoke in public about what had happened; members of the pastor's family still lived in town and maintained ties to the church.

Was this pastor from Seaview Church's fairly recent past a hero or a villain? It seemed to the members on the renewal project that the congregation was not clear on this question. Certainly its silence over the years indicated that this pastorate was something of an embarrassment to the congregation. Yet his continued presence in the community confused the matter: if he were indeed an out-and-out villain, the church would have to ignore him completely. This option must have seemed out of the question, in light of his still living in the community.

Seaview's members participating in the renewal training process agreed that the history of this pastoral tenure had had a demoralizing effect upon its congregation. They also agreed that they wanted to do something to help break the grip of this bad memory. How to go about it was the question. First, they decided that this bit of history could not be made the focus of attention—at least not right away. In sharing with the church board the insights and ideas gained from the training, the team of leaders decided to promote a churchwide story-sharing activity. An explanation and instructions for the event would be well-publicized in advance, encouraging both longtime and newer members to participate. Questions and directions were carefully prepared and worded. The team requested and secured the facilitation services of a well-regarded church member with experience in group dynamics. Using this process, the renewal team prepared to help its congregation work through the symbolic meaning of this pastor's influence on their life.

The Congregation's Rituals and Ceremonies

For churches, the anthropological concepts of ritual and ceremony immediately relate—but in more ways than at first might be supposed. As mentioned earlier in the chapter, congregations engage in certain regular ceremonies and rituals and encourage rituals of personal devotion. Weekly worship combines the congregation's ecclesiastical tradition with some idiosyncratic elements that grow out of their particular experience. Some churches, for instances, might sing "Happy Birthday" once a month in Sunday worship to those celebrating birthdays in that month. Worship is ceremony, since it publicly symbolizes through a series of corporate behaviors something about what is important to that congregation.

At this point, it is legitimate to raise the question of the efficacy of a church's explicitly religious ritual and ceremony. Is it doing what it is "supposed to?" Are the persons in the sanctuary "getting it?" The phrase "empty ritual" has been used in recent years to criticize what is perceived as a lack of genuine spiritual interest and energy during congregational worship.

From the perspective of the concepts of ritual and ceremony, this is unfortunate. Rituals and ceremonies develop in cultures as ways of ordering and symbolizing life's significant realities as they are understood. What qualifies as significant, even for the culture of a congregation, will not always be confined to the obvious elements of worship. Yet it certainly makes sense that worship is one place for a congregation to enact its self-understanding with awareness, conviction, and vigor. When those responsible for a congregation's regular worship life approach their task primarily on the basis of acceptable routine, the theological elements of their beliefs, myths, and stories will diminish. Over time, such a congregation will not remember who it was, even though it thinks it knows—and that its memory still carries power.

We have been speaking in two distinguishable, but yet intertwined, ways about ritual and ceremony: the formal and the informal, the explicit and the implicit, and—for churches—the sacred and the common. Again we return to the claim that many features of culture are interdependent, and so also with ritual and ceremony. Attempts to change established elements of a congregation's rituals and ceremonies easily can become counterproductive. Pastors who begin a new call or appointment are often tempted to begin "monkeying around" with the Sunday liturgy before they even know the names of the church members. I have heard many stories from pastors and seminary students alike about controversies sparked early in a pastoral tenure regarding worship.

One Methodist student pastor spent her first few months in a new appointment trying to convince the congregation that its liturgy was not true to the denomination's discipline. The congregation interpreted its new pastor's efforts as a lack of interest in and respect for them. Technically, she was right: the congregation followed an order of service bearing scant resemblance to their denominational tradition. Yet this familiar form of worship did symbolize certain deep, significant aspects of the congregation's life together. Some of those aspects might not be as healthy as others, and they might need to change if the congregation was to seek a stronger faith and witness. Yet their new pastor's insistence on immediately replacing those rituals and ceremonies was impeding her efforts to help the congregation.

A similar situation developed within a declining Protestant congregation whose urban neighborhood had become heavily Roman Catholic. The congregation's new pastor loved traditional liturgy and enjoyed borrowing rituals from the Mass as he officiated over the Lord's Supper. Many members of the congregations, however, were not enamored. They felt that their new pastor's enthusiasm was misplaced. With a strong history in the free church tradition, this dwindling but persistent church wanted to maintain its identity in the midst of the religious changes in its neighborhood. Being Protestant for them meant looking and acting the way that Protestants traditionally have looked and acted. Communion liturgy that "looked Roman Catholic" violated their sense of identity. In discussions with the worship committee, the pastor sometimes would plead, "But there are reasons!" His reasons, however, persuaded few of the members of this century-plus congregation: to them, the symbolic power of their own traditional communion ceremony was too great to relinquish. Such is the power of rituals, symbols, and ceremony.

Earlier in this chapter, we looked at how two congregations in East Park had been prepared skillfully for merger. Pastor Tod's leadership was not complete without symbol and ceremony. Planning for the first Sunday of worship together was deliberate and careful. The decision already had been made on which building to sell to the city and which one to use. On the appointed day, Pentecost Sunday, the members of the congregation that was giving up its building processed down the streets to their new home. They carried with them several objects from their former sanctuary to be used in their new one: the flags, the pulpit Bible, paraments, and communion ware. This public event told their neighborhood that a new congregation had been born. Every year on Pentecost Sunday, the new East Park church celebrates its birthday along with the traditional "birthday of the church." That processional Sunday carried many rich memories and moments to close one chapter of congregational life and open another.

Not all a congregation's rituals and ceremonies bear the same kind of significance as Pentecost Sunday does for East Park—although they can be just as strong. A fellowship committee at one church begins preparing the coffee and cookies for "coffee hour" about twenty minutes before worship begins. It takes less than that amount of time to set up the coffee makers, which have automatic thermostats, and lay out the cookies. But the tradition at this church for years has been that those who have coffee duty that day stand around chatting in the kitchen during the entire service! Similar rituals can be found in many congregations.

Liminality and Communitas in Congregations

While most of the concepts discussed in this chapter are fairly or readily recognizable, liminality and communitas might seem unfamiliar. Particularly for established congregations, the notion that they would go through an experience creating uncertainty and possibly a new identity sounds undesirable. Yet, over the life of a congregation, liminality and communitas describe significant and often transforming experiences.

At the formal level of ritual and ceremony, consider baptism, confirmation, wedding, and funeral. All four of these events occur in churches, two primarily so. Each one of them marks a transition from one status to another. In baptism, the person is sealed by the Holy Spirit as part of the people of God. In confirmation, the young persons confirm their baptismal vows and accept responsibility for full, active participation in the congregation. In a wedding, two persons pledge before God to begin a life of particular love and responsibilities. At a funeral, a person's life on earth is remembered and his or her everlasting assurance affirmed.

For most Christian traditions, too, these ceremonies involve the community of believers in some way—making pledges, acting as witnesses, celebrating. In other words, the transition for the persons occurs within the larger context of the church. There is a certain built-in "protection" to the process, because the larger community has passed that way before. Ideally, then, the liminal nature of, say, confirmation and marriage leads in the church to communitas experience with other members.

There are other ways in which liminality and communitas occur and can occur in a congregation. Some of the most common forms are with youth ministry activities and camping. The creation in modernity of the phenomenon that is called adolescence led in the late nineteenth century to church programs aimed at teenagers. The youth group as an institution assumes teenage liminality at the macrocultural level. Youth ministries that are deemed "successful" often do so on the foundation of a strong experience of communitas—"we're all in this together." Because of the strong age segmentation in the macroculture, it takes deliberate and considerable effort for a church to move youth ministry out of a youth group model that is mostly introspective and self-serving. To argue that youth need to be more integrated into the life of the overall church community, however, does not diminish the fact that strong communitas can be provided in youth groups.

The same is true for church camps and conferences, only here the age factor is broader and the setting is more evidently liminal. Camps and conferences bring church people out of their usual routine and status, giving them a new status that, albeit temporary, tends to be fairly egalitarian. Exposure to new persons, to familiar persons in different settings, to new perspectives and experiences, as well as taking place in a special location all contribute to the liminality. "How can we take this back to our churches?" is a common question raised at the end of camps and conferences that recognizes not only the positive communitas but also the desire to share the new insights and practices at home.

At the same time, liminality and communitas can involve risk, and sometimes congregations are not willing to engage in such a process. For example, since the 1960s, many denominations have encouraged the inclusion of children into full participation in Sunday worship. Very few congregations have been able, even if they were willing, to change that part of their culture. It means changing the status of worship itself; it requires that adults interact with children in the sanctuary in different ways; it means that what was orderly, predictable, and comfortable now will be less certain. These issues appear to many congregations as not worth the risk, which would be so verbalized in less revealing and more "acceptable" terms.

Yet there are biblical resources easily at hand to encourage ventures in liminality and communitas. The long story beginning with Abraham and Sarah, through the entry into the promised land, is a story about creating community while being "betwixt and between." The period of the exile was a time of tremendous uncertainty, in which a remnant held onto its former identity even as they reshaped it. Jesus called men and women who left their homes, entering liminality, and developed communitas along the way. So also do the first churches experience faith together, as interpreted in Acts.

As a pair of concepts, liminality and communitas give church leaders some handles for understanding the implications of change. Change is a given reality today, and it continues to accelerate. Our churches are populated by a generation of people who tend to view change as positive only if it is incremental. Church leaders who understand the power of transition and of reshaping community in transition are better equipped to design creative possibilities that the congregation might actually embrace.

UNDERSTANDING AND LEADING YOUR VILLAGE

So, then, what had the young pastor at the beginning of this chapter failed to learn about the church that he was serving? He had not learned their culture; even more pointedly, he did not see the congregation as a village. His implicit view of churches had not helped him understand the larger scale of the phenomenon with which he was dealing.

In reflecting upon the material in this chapter, we should be able to discover a number of ways to apply it to congregations. In broad terms, for instance, we can appreciate their subtle complexity as an intersection of cultures. Influences from the particular congregation's local community, its region of the country, and the wider macroculture enter the church door. There they mix, shape, and sometimes cross with the congregation's own distinctive culture. The ways in which this intersection occurs tell us a lot about that congregation.

Another benefit of using cultural anthropology to interpret congregations is its focused way of relating individuals and communities. Clifford Geertz, the famous anthropologist, has written that it is impossible to find a person who is not affected by specific practices from specific settings, what Geertz calls "the customs of particular places."[15] For American churches, one of the implications of this insight should be clear: that human beings are not as individualistic as the macrocultural American myth promotes. Persons bear the marks of habits, values, patterns from somewhere and sometime, even when they seek out new ones to replace the early ones.

Practically speaking, then, the challenge for churches is to make the most of their nature as cultural entities. By this, I do not mean that churches simply say, "Well, this is the way we are, and that's that." Rather, church leaders can learn to think about their congregations using concepts like those in this chapter. This kind of method is not new, since seminaries have been training ministerial students with psychological concepts, theories, and methods for decades. A pastor and lay leader who "know their way around the village" are much more likely to discern its needs and shape an approach to guide and strengthen the church.

Church Leader as Shaman

One anthropological concept that can be used as a metaphor for this kind of leadership is the *shaman*. Technically, a shaman is defined as one who is "socially recognized as having supernatural powers that are used on behalf of clients for a variety of activities."[16] For our purposes, this definition can be adapted to something like, "one to whom the congregation has granted some of its power." In villages, a shaman is a person who the village knows can do special things in its midst, things that it needs, even if it does not always enjoy the medicine. In one sense, then, pastors especially need to learn what it takes to be granted such power (mana) by the congregation being served. We will see in the next chapter how to adapt this kind of "symbolic" leadership for congregations, as we consider them in terms of organizations with culture.

Shamanlike effectiveness calls for skills that the missionary in the village of watermelons did not understand. Sometime following his sudden demise, a second missionary appeared in their village. He also began his contact with them by asking the elders questions. Before long, the new missionary's attention was drawn to the somewhat foreboding hill in the distance. "And what is over there?"

Again the elders gave their veiled answer. "Our people never go that way. Too dangerous." The missionary persisted until he was told of the watermelon patch and their fear of its supposed deadly powers. Unlike his predecessor, however, the new missionary showed no surprise or impatience. Instead, he sat quietly for a few moments, pondering their comments. Then he quietly and innocently asked, "When was the last time anyone from your village actually *saw* the watermelon patch?"

Elders began looking at each other with puzzled expressions. No one could remember, and the chief told the missionary so. He sat quietly again. Then, looking at them intently, he asked, "Would the chief object if I went to the hill and peeked over, just to see what I could see?"

His question hit the village like a small current of electricity. Even the women and children standing inside the entrances of the huts jumped back a little when they heard it. All eyes turned to the chief. Sensing the anxiety, the missionary spoke firmly but soothingly, "I give you my word that I will not do anything to put your village in danger." Moments passed. Then the chief said, "The watermelons possess great power. Do not let any of it touch you. And be quick!"

So, as the entire village watched from their huts, the missionary walked quietly toward the hill. He crouched at its base, turned back to face the village for a moment, and waved. A moment later, the chief waved back. The missionary started up the hill, carefully choosing every step so as to avoid making any sound. Halfway up, he crouched again and waved back to the village; again, the chief waved back. A minute later, the missionary had reached the crest of the hill and was now crawling on his stomach. As he lifted his head to look over the crest, heads poked out of the huts down below. Hiding behind a bush, the missionary took one long steady look and then carefully backed himself away from the crest. Out of view from the top of the hill, he stood up and retraced his steps. The elders were standing, waiting for him when he reached the village center.

After a few moments of visual perusal, they decided that the missionary did not get touched by any of the watermelon power. So they invited him to sit down and, as he did so, they asked him many questions. That night, after the young children went to bed, drummers played while the missionary told and retold his adventure of peeking over the crest of the hill.

A few days later, the missionary was sitting again with the elders. After hearing more about their way of life, the missionary asked, "May I have the chief's permission to take a few of the men, whom the chief himself selects, to peek over the crest of the hill?"

It was only a second before the chief replied: "I have been waiting for you to request this expedition of me, and I have decided who will go with you. But only just as you yourself ventured." So the small party visited the hill, while the village watched as before. That night, drummers played while several men told of their adventure. There were smiles around the circle.

A week later, the missionary asked to go over the crest of the hill by himself, so he could get a closer look at the watermelons—hiding behind bushes, to be sure. The request was granted, with some trepidation. Upon his return, the missionary was first "screened" as before, and again the stories were told at night by drum, as children strained from their bed mats to hear.

Within the next month, the missionary made several more trips, the final one being an expedition with a large band of the men right into the patch, to pick watermelons off the vine and smash them against the ground. Their jubilation was so raucous that it could be heard back at the village. That night, a festival-style event was held; the women painted themselves; the men danced; the children laughed and played the new village game, "watermelon smashing;" the missionary received a walking stick from the chief; and a new story took shape. It was the story of the pale shaman sent by the gods to destroy the mana of the watermelon patch.

It is our challenge as church leaders to be as wise as this missionary was, with the culture that he learned, respected, and helped to transform.

FOUR

N O T   A   "N E C E S S A R Y   E V I L"

Congregation as Locus of Exchange

BILLBOARD THEOLOGY

It was like so many other small towns along the smooth shoreline. Views of the lake peeked out from snatches of open light that seemed, from the seat of a moving vehicle on the highway, to stagger themselves between clumps of trees. Summer homes crowded into space not taken up by residences and occasional fields. For those who lived, as well as those who vacationed, in this town, it was a place to get away from the rat race.

What, then, was so strange about one of the few billboards next to the road approaching town? Its picture, a lighthouse, certainly fit into the romantic maritime theme that residents and visitors alike warmly embraced. Passersby could have expected an advertisement for boat sales, a restaurant, the chamber of commerce, a museum, or the like. Instead, what they read as they slowed down near the city limits sign was:

Just around the corner . . . *Find light for your life! Join us each Sunday!* Ascension Episcopal Church, 123 Main Street, Laketown, 123-456-7890

Now, certain church traditions have used billboards for many years, quoting their pet Bible verses. Sometimes, too, churches use billboards to draw attention to themselves. What was so unusual about the billboard quoted above is that it was for a mainstream Protestant church!

Ascension Episcopal Church is not alone. A growing number of churches that many people formerly would have considered too "nice and proper" to advertise are doing just that. Billboards, telephone directories, newspapers, and flyers distributed by hand, on windows, and in the mail—more and more congregations are promoting themselves in the public arena. Similar to the business world, congregations are beginning to offer the public a wide variety of services that they claim will benefit the "taker." In years gone by, pastors often viewed such tactics as anathema. Increasingly, however, church officials view marketing as necessary, perhaps a "necessary evil."[1]

In this chapter, we will explore the life of congregations from a vantage point that does not even register on many a churchperson's radar: economics. Our intention is not to claim that congregations and businesses are identical in every way when it comes to money and resources, or that churches that simply imitate what smart companies do will see a rise in membership and giving. We will begin to sort our way through the similarities and differences between churches and other organizations in chapter 6. One of the emphases there will be to recognize the unavoidable relationship between organizations and their environments. Since congregations are indeed organizations, and since the larger environment is so heavily influenced by economic factors, it makes sense to think about congregations in at least some economic terms.

This chapter, hence, will focus upon two key concepts of our modern and postmodern economic system: market and capital. Our goal here is not to write another textbook on economics! Rather, we will learn a little about how these concepts emerged, how they are defined, what related concepts elaborate upon them, how these concepts taken together help us understand religion today, and what they could help church leaders do more effectively and faithfully.

THE CONCEPT AND PLACE OF "MARKET"

We begin with the concept that is perhaps the one more evident to us in our daily lives: the notion of market. You might be surprised to find out that, for some time now, a number of scholars of American religion have been interpreting their research using images from economics.

Some Historical Background

Phrases such as "marketing skill," "rational choice," "supply side," and "entrepreneurs" dot more recent scholarly literature on religion from both social scientists and historians.[2] You might be equally surprised to realize that the forces that helped to create the economic system that now dominates today's world took centuries to develop.[3] That is to say, the practice of free enterprise and the use of capital for investment, as basic features of economy, were able to emerge in the West through a long and complex interaction of political, religious, and social factors. Some of those factors and forces are particularly helpful in understanding the relation of today's religion to economic realities.

The Voluntary Association

One of the most significant phenomena to emerge in history is known in scholarly circles as "the voluntary association." As we saw in chapter 1, this is the notion that human beings can affiliate with other persons and groups, of like interest and goal, free from restraints or sanctions imposed by religion, government or birth.[4] This concept has become so much a part of modern, especially American, thinking that it is hard for some readers to realize that it has experienced a long and mostly subversive history. Its roots can be traced to the ancient Greek city-state and a few centuries later to the young Christian movement. Its expression religiously, economically, and politically is seen in Europe during the early stages of the Renaissance on all major fronts—politically (founding new settlements), religiously (new orders), and economically (rise of merchant class). Voluntary associations as a concept in practice appears again with irrevocable force during the sixteenth-century Protestant Reformation; new religious movements took hold and began to significantly shape community and economic life.

Indeed, it was the religiously inspired impetus for free association that sparked much of the early colonization of North America.[5]

State control of church eventually gave way, in the colonies-turned-United States, to no established church. The implications of this change in religious and political affiliation was significant in at least two ways. One was that persons could now choose not to be members of a church; they could voluntarily associate or not associate with one. Secondly, since the state did not maintain an established church, the means of funding churches necessarily shifted. Rather than receiving tax funds to support their work, congregations—being voluntary associations—now had to provide their own financial support. Hence, one symbol of the new, voluntary church became the offering plate!

It is only fair to note that "disestablishment"—that is, separation of church and state, which stimulated the expansion of the voluntary association—was not supported by everyone. Thomas Hobbes, for instance,[6] argued in the mid-seventeenth century that only the monarch of the country had the right to dictate persons' religious affiliation. His perspective, however, was losing against a new tide in history. Yet Hobbes, prophetically, also realized that allowing religion to associate freely from regulation by, and sanction from, government would create a snowball effect. Other kinds of voluntary associations, promoting other kinds of freedoms, would emerge. As we in the modern world so well know, Hobbes was right. Today there are so many professional, recreational, intellectual, political, and who-knows-what other kind of voluntary associations that we can hardly keep track of them all!

We thus can come to appreciate the way in which the concept of voluntary association, as it took gradually form in Western history, helped to lay the groundwork for what we experience today in the "free market."

Market and Religion

Simply stated, a market is a *means by which parties exchange goods or services through some form of payment*. Obviously, markets have existed for much of human experience, but the ability to influence terms of exchange—not to mention the nature and type of the goods themselves—usually was restricted by governments.[7] Economic "choice," to a large degree, was a long time coming.

Yet this does not mean that market and religion have converged only in very recent years. Indeed, some scholars now argue[8] that key factors in the late eighteenth and early nineteenth centuries encouraged the American religious scene to create, in a real sense, its own market forces. These forces involved some level of competition, as awakenings and revivals were led by people in several denominational traditions—Methodist, Presbyterian, Congregational, Episcopal, Baptist, Reformed, Lutheran and even Unitarian.[9] The effects of this market competition seem to have created a long-term benefit for religion, and not just in the United States. One researcher[10] concludes that countries with a range of church groups available also have a higher percentage of both religious belief and attendance than countries in which one religious institution overshadows any others.

Hence, for those interested in evangelism and church growth, perhaps more than a blessing is necessary. It might be wise as well to paraphrase the popular saying from the "Star Wars" movie trilogy: "May the market be with you!" If nothing else, a tongue-in-cheek paraphrase like this one could serve to remind ourselves of something central to the gospel: the Word has to fall on somebody's ears, and preferably it will be somebody who might be receptive.

"Church Shopping"

These historical observations serve to indicate the kind of momentum that already was in place on the American religious scene during the twentieth century. What we are witnessing at the beginning of a new century and millennium is a further intensification of this pattern toward religion as a market for choice. This intensification has been well-documented and discussed in the literature, most of which recognizes that the 1960s mark a major watershed era in American religion.[11] Attendance patterns for baby boomers—those youth who faded away from church in the '60s—has not picked up since then, as many churchpeople thought it would. They are instead choosing for the most part to stay away. This is especially true for boomers raised in mainstream Protestant churches, where church involvement became one of a number of acceptable options for one's activity.[12]

Of course, we realize that this attitude and practice has led to a long-standing numerical decline in most of the mainstream Protestant denominations. What is important to highlight at this point is that it is a result in part of a historically new climate that allows, even encourages, individual choice. For mainstream Protestantism at least, the paramount feature for church attendance has become choice—more than denominational allegiance, more than a sense of need or duty, more than routine.[13] This exercise of choice means that, for mainstream churches, the notion of "market" now functions as a de facto byword. American religion operates in a marketplace, where consumers select churches based on how well their emphases and activities meet the particular consumer's identified needs. This marketplace functions in spite of the presence in these denominations of a (declining) number of longtime, aging members motivated by allegiance.[14]

It would be a serious mistake, however, to dismiss this growing consumer attitude toward religion as merely cavalier. Americans in particular live virtually engulfed by a plethora of choice, at every level. While there are times when the amount and degree of choice bewilders us, it is almost impossible to escape the daily need to make selections.[15] Although choice in religion is seen in its most "pure" form in mainstream Protestantism, it nonetheless affects conservative Protestants and Roman Catholics as well.[16] People in today's world must make choices, and religion increasingly has become one of many such choices.

Not only this, but the evidence indicates that today's church consumers are sophisticated "shoppers."[17] It is not the case that they know the Bible or theology well; on the other hand, they are pretty focused about what they expect the church of their choice to provide for them. It is not enough simply that the church holds weekly worship: "How well does the music appeal to their tastes? Is there a nursery and Sunday school? What is taught and how are the children treated? Does the sermon touch on matters that affect my life? How do the people here treat me? What will they expect of me?" High on the list for church shoppers are expectations of style and quality.

The shopper metaphor also helps us see that church consumers also tend to choose the ways in which they will participate in a church. Like a customer walking through a department store, seeking out particular departments from which to select and purchase certain items, so today's church consumer tends to be selective about which areas of the church's life in which to engage. Except in very conservative or sectarian congregations, an "all-or-nothing" stance on church attendance is not realistic for a consumer-conscious congregation to demand.

THE CHURCH IN THE MARKETPLACE

These observations about the influence of market factors upon American religion, disturbing as they might be to some, lead us to ponder their implications for churches.[18] For one thing, they suggest that churches should give close attention to what they are providing. What kind of programming does the church offer? Any kind of activity that the church schedules, plans, and sponsors can be a place where members and visitors have certain needs met. These activities certainly would include such traditional, mainstay activities as worship, educational classes and groups, social events for fun and community-building, and help/outreach to people in need. For a congregation seeking to welcome and support new people, programming very likely will need to be adapted and/or increased.

Emmaus Church anticipated the arrival of its new pastor, Rev. Billings, since a conflict surrounding its previous pastor had resulted in reduced membership, attendance, and giving. Rev. Billings, a conscientious pastor, quickly moved to address the situation. Within a few months, the church began offering a Saturday afternoon worship service. The Catholic church in town some years ago had instituted a mass at that time of the week, and Emmaus was hoping to attract a similar clientele: people who, for reasons of work, children's sport schedules, informality, or choice, would like the option of worshiping on other than a Sunday morning. A year later, the congregation negotiated for a day care center to be started in their spacious and well-situated building. The initial public marketing for the center went out as a flyer in an issue of the town's weekly newspaper. Again, the hope was partly that young families using the day care center, and who had no church ties, would become interested in Emmaus and visit worship.

Both of these initiatives by Emmaus Church indicate a willingness to provide programming to meet needs in the community. In the consumer marketplace of American society, such an effort demonstrates creativity and a willingness to risk. Before Emmaus undertook these new programs, they would have wanted their church board to consider the following questions:

- What needs in our town currently are not being fully met?
- How might we respond to these needs?
- Who will be served?

- How can we reach them with information on what we have to offer?
- How will we engage persons who are interested in our church, all the way through from their first inquiry to participation and hopefully membership?

Each one of these questions grows out of an awareness of marketing principles and realities. Many congregations have occasion to brush up on at least the given conditions of their surroundings, since a number of denominations require their congregations in pastoral transition to undergo a self-study. This study includes a collection of census-type demographic data about the church's community. Many of these data help to define the church's potential "market," but ironically, congregational officials often do not engage them in any serious way. Many self-study groups will complete their analysis of their market area without ever asking themselves how this information affects them.

However, even more fundamental to the willing congregation's consideration of its market is the question of purpose: What is our church's vision of itself and its mission in this community, from which decisions about programming and marketing are made?

If a congregation's vision is not clear or strong, its decisions about marketing and programming will be hampered, because those decisions by default will be made on the basis of congregational assumptions that are implicit. Just because a committee might be able to agree upon a new market-driven program does not mean that the committee members are motivated by the same reasons. Even if such reasons are expressed and held in common, they might not be linked to a common congregational vision.

For a congregation to think of its life in terms of market is one way that could lead it also to think about overall purpose and identity. There is no guarantee that this will happen, however. Many congregations find it much easier to make plans, prepare details, and run programs than they do to articulate their picture of what God calls them to be and do. Even a thorough "textbook" of marketing for congregations makes this point. It asserts that "More important than marketing, or any management approach, are the spirit of the congregation and spirituality of the leaders and workers. . . . Most needed . . . is vision."[19]

In other words, marketing—like anything else that a church might consider—is not a panacea. It does not magically "fix" what is wrong in a church. It can, however, be a tool, a very useful and effective tool, in the hands of church leaders who understand its place in their congregation's vision for ministry.

CAPITAL

When many of us hear the word, "capital," we might first think of the names of cities in the fifty states that we tried to memorize as a child! If our attention is drawn to capital as a concept from economics, though, many of us might invoke a much less clear image. My guess is that, since most of us are exposed to it every day, we are fairly familiar with marketing—its vast array of techniques, tools, and practices. Our image of capital, however, might be nothing more than something associated with what goes on in a skyscraper with a name like "IBM" or "First National" on it. If this is true, then our view of the concept of capital is, if not inaccurate, then somewhat limited.

A Definition

A simple definition of capital would be that it is *any and all kinds of resources that can be used to make something that someone could use*. This definition sounds general and broad, and that is its intention. When we consider the way that capital has been most commonly understood and applied over the last several generations, we think of factories, machines, workers, substantial financial outlay,[20] and material products such as clothing, food, houses, automobiles, furniture, computers, and the like. These concrete items do indeed illustrate much, but not necessarily all, of what encompasses the notion.

A Congregation's Capital

Many, if not most, congregations possess capital in categories that are similar to those of a profit-making corporation, even though the congregation's most basic normative goals will differ from those of a business. Often the most evident form of a congregation's capital are its buildings. They, of course, are designed to be used for such activities as worship, education, fellowship, community service events (for example, voting, blood drives, twelve-step groups), and other purposes. In order to possess a building, a congregation must raise money; make mortgage, insurance, and utilities payments; provide for the facility's maintenance and upkeep; and so on. This requires sufficient finances over the life of the building, finances that usually are supported largely by regular contributions from members and friends.

Congregations also often own land. They usually own the lot upon which their building stands, but they also could own a parsonage, a parking lot, and space used for recreation or other programmatic or aesthetic purpose (one church has developed a combination meditation garden and columbarium; it allows members the opportunity to contemplate things in the midst of the communion of saints). Ownership of real estate involves the congregation in necessary, even if tedious, legal matters with various levels of government.

Of course, along with real estate come the necessary furniture and other property/equipment by which the facilities become even more useful. Here again congregations parallel business, for they use such technology as telephones, door locks, crash bars (required by fire code), file cabinets, desks, computers, alarm systems, and so forth. Such items look or function in congregations in ways almost identical to like items in business—unlike items such as pews, baptismals, pulpits, hymnals, and so on, that are understood to be distinctly religious in nature. It would be very difficult to imagine a congregation today functioning well without this type of equipment. It is one primary symbol of being a "clay jar" in the twenty-first-century West.

Another one of those symbols is money. Besides real estate and furnishings/equipment as capital, today's congregation is forced to deal in the money economy of our capitalist system. When congregations are just getting started, they rely almost entirely upon the regular offerings and pledges of members and friends. As time goes by, then, congregations often are able to create savings accounts for various purposes not dictated by daily operations and expenses: memorials, maintenance, renovations/additions, scholarships for camps, conferences, and schooling. As more time goes by, some congregations find themselves in the position of receiving from a member's estate a substantial gift, to be used as endowment. In other words, the intent of this money is to earn money that the congregation can then utilize, often for specified purposes. Not infrequently, a further source of money comes from rental fees paid by outside groups for use of certain parts of the congregation's facilities (parking, gymnasium, nonmember weddings, social hall/kitchen, and the like).

This quick rundown of common types of concrete capital serves to visualize for us the many, and sometimes complex, ways that congregations are involved in a capital economy. In most cases, too, congregations find that the best way to account for all this capital is through a common practice in the business world, budgeting. The money that a congregation raises gets used in two basic ways: to support its programs and activities, and to help its operational efficiency. Churches spend money to use facilities, whether to rent or to pay a mortgage; to pay for electricity, telephone, water, and other utilities; to operate an office with equipment, supplies, and a secretary; to insure property; to hire musical personnel for worship services; to pay a pastor to lead worship, preach, counsel, help plan and lead various programs, teach, respond to crisis, assist church committees, and so on. Many denominations require their congregations to audit their financial records annually, at least internally, to keep accountability regular and aboveboard. The trust by which members contribute money to the congregation needs to be maintained.

As a congregation continues to exist over the years, its participation in our world's capital economy inevitably tends to increase. Long-term survival tends to place certain kinds of demands upon an organization that seemed only dim, exciting possibilities at the outset. These possibilities-turned-demands usually involve accumulation of assets. Stated the other way, it would be very difficult, if not impossible, in this era for a new congregation to survive for long if it refused to interact with some forms of capital. Even countercultural, alternative forms of Christian witness are subject to this inertia toward participation with resources and exchange.

Struggling with an "Anticapital" Ideal

One historical example,[21] although from medieval times, illustrates this economic point. Centuries ago, a young Italian man literally walked away from his family's wealth to found a religious order based upon simplicity, itinerancy, and not owning property. The movement was popular enough to have survived its founder's death, but it was not possible to maintain his standards as purely as

Francis of Assisi and his followers had done in his day. As a matter of fact, one mere century following his death, Francis' order was the wealthiest in Europe, in need of the same kind of reform that led Francis to eschew property to begin with!

This struggle for a Christian community to keep the weight of material possessions from diverting its purposes can be found, on occasion, in today's consumer-driven world, too. One young congregation, New Way Christian Fellowship, tried to exist without buying or constructing a facility. Born out of the social upheavals of the 1960s, this well-educated group of independent Christians took seriously Jesus' words to the seventy who were sent out to the villages (Luke 10:1–12). They were told to travel light on their mission. This new, socially conscious and world-conscious congregation wanted their life and mission to be as unencumbered by concerns over ownership of property as possible. For three decades, they met in the buildings of other religious groups, arranging leases to use space during off-hours.

Gradually, though, the question came up about having a permanent home. There was just about no way to guarantee a long-standing location, with freedom to use it as they pleased, without the congregation biting the bullet and purchasing or building its own facility. Old-liners were reluctant to give their support, but the weight of the other arguments became difficult to dispute. So New Way Christian Fellowship began the tedious process of creating its own home; it was a process that would engage them in many contacts and interactions with elements of our capitalist economy. When they finally closed the sale of an existing church building and held their first services in it, their life had become more complicated—but also more permanent.

Skyway Methodist Church went through a different, and unfortunately more common, situation with its capital. Also a young congregation, Skyway had constructed a church facility within a few years of its founding, a modest but beautiful structure that blends in well with its surroundings. Most of the money for construction was borrowed from the denomination, with a generous payment plan arranged. As a consequence of conflict over the pastor, however, a number of members left the small church, which was left facing bills that now were hard to meet. Payments on their building loan fell behind—first months, then years behind.

When the denominational processes finally helped stabilize Skyway and send in a permanent pastor, many people had forgotten about the young congregation's substantial debt. Two years after the new pastor arrived, the outstanding loan was uncovered. The pastor, the trustees, and the administrative council were all stunned. Then, as they considered the gravity of their situation, their spirits fell. Could they survive this seemingly insurmountable financial challenge?

Skyway's new pastor was experienced in dealing with conflict in congregations. He led the trustees to plan and implement a capital campaign. After two years of meeting campaign pledges, the congregation had reduced its mortgage by two-thirds. The end of their debt was in sight! Morale within the congregation began to rise again; in casual conversations and church meetings, members began to say things like, "Now we know that we can survive!" Skyway's church leaders were ready to take on new challenges. Now they were more confident that they had something positive to offer church seekers in their attractive, growing community.

The point of this section on capital is not to claim that congregations become capitalistic ventures alongside businesses and corporations. Yet, it is nonetheless true that many of the basic elements of a capitalist economy—resources of various kinds, production, goods, exchange, and the media thereof—have a direct bearing upon the life of today's congregations. This is especially true for congregations in those parts of the world where Western forms of economic practice are present. We swim in a capitalistic stream, and it is pretty hard to swim against it constantly!

A "HUMAN" APPLICATION

Some economists translate the notion of capital also into human terms. Seen in this light, "human capital" consists of *the ways that persons apply their own experience, skills, energy, and interests toward certain activities and programs, with the expectation that such an "investment" will pay "dividends" to them.* To an economist, human capital is a concept that helps to measure relationships among several factors:

- what persons have to offer to some object of participation
- what worth they ascribe to particular activities and achievements

- what worth the particular "market" places on the person's contributions
- what benefits the person perceives and hence hopes to derive from the activities
- what "stores" of human capital accrue to which persons in a system and why
- how those stores of capital are drawn upon and for what purposes

This kind of analysis does not lend itself readily to the same kind of precision as, say, the cost-effective analysis of a cookie factory. Even if the notion of capital were to be taken in this context only as a metaphor, it helps us understand that resources, exchange, expectation, achievement, and negotiation can and does have a human dimension and application.

Take the example of modern education. When I was in high school in the 1960s, I vividly remember a clever and impressionable television community service spot. It showed a young man preparing with determination to walk into a large office building, as though he were heading toward a job interview. Instead, he gets stuck inside the revolving door, which spins him around faster and faster, until he is thrown back out on the sidewalk, not knowing what hit him. All the while, the voice narration explains that trying to get a good job without staying in school is like getting stuck in a revolving door. The spot ended with a short statement that I have remembered for years: "To get a good job, get a good education."

My generation grew up imbued with the belief that adequate formal education was the one investment that would open up all the doors that we could seek. I contemplated with mute disbelief the large number of high school classmates in my small town who did not make this investment of a college degree. Many of them, I must have concluded, were not aiming very high in life.

Then along came the economic roller coasters of the 1970s and 1980s. Suddenly, the promise of interesting work, good money, and ever-broadening opportunity seemed somewhat elusive. Preparing one's human capital for a complex, challenging, but rewarding professional career—based on the credentials bestowed by college and graduate degrees—was a high investment to make, when the jobs were scarcer. One older church member who is especially interested in youth once said to me, "It's harder and harder to convince these kids to stay in college, when they hear how rough the job market is when they get through!" The investment of even our human capital is a risk, in which anticipated rewards and benefits must be weighed against the odds of eventual achievement.

The Congregation: Object of Human Capital

One of my favorite biblical texts speaks in its own ancient terms about the value and purpose of human capital. In his first letter to the squabbling band of believers in Corinth, Paul spoke on a number of topics of which he heard they needed guidance. One of those topics was the role of the Holy Spirit in the life and experience of the community of faith. Chapter twelve is a passage that perhaps has been only vaguely understood in modern times, certainly not utilized much beyond ordination services. Here, however, Paul lays out an understanding of God's participation with human beings that can be interpreted insightfully in terms of human capital.

Paul discusses gifts of the Spirit, which are bestowed by God, at God's bidding, to the several members of the household of faith. Using the metaphor of a body, Paul emphasizes that what God provides has as its purpose the benefit of the whole. When the Spirit "gifts" the people, there is no place made for individual grandstanding and acclaim. The object of the many gifts is to do good for the church: "To each is given the manifestation of the Spirit for the common good" (1 Cor. 12:7).

For believers, then, gifts of the Spirit become—in a sense—part of their human capital. Our focus here is not upon the specific gifts that Paul lists, but upon the dynamic exchanges between the Spirit, the individual, and the community. What believers have to invest are abilities given to them, yes, but to exercise through the body of believers. In other words, their investment of human capital into the congregation pays off for them as the congregation benefits from what they provide. For the church, the dividends to individual participation are most important (if not always most evident) in its public arena.

This insight operates in its negative or opposite terms, sometimes dramatically. Churches that thwart the efforts of church members to share their gifts can expect to lose members, especially those who are newer; the latter have less invested than longtime members and—although they will experience noticeable loss by leaving—often conclude that they would have more to lose by remaining. Conversely, longtime members who do not perceive dividends to their church investment usually remain but curtail their involvement.

Such was the case with All Souls' Church, whose Sunday school enrollment plummeted from fifty in 1980 to only three five years later, even though economic and social conditions in town had stayed stable. Controversy gradually grew over the effectiveness of All Souls' new pastor, hired in part to attract families with children. Several of these young families had joined and become quite active early in the new pastoral tenure. As time went by, however, virtually all of these families left the congregation, although most of them had remained in town. Their reasons for leaving All Souls' were twofold: they came to dislike the pastor's leadership style; and they concluded that the congregation overall was not open to new people and ideas. After a period of sustained tension, the pastor resigned. Many longtime members then were hoping that the newer ones who had left would come back. None of them did. Conversations with several of the departed ones indicated that they were so frustrated, hurt, and tired from the controversy that they could not return. They had overextended their human capital and, in their eyes, had lost it. To risk again to such an extent was not worth it to them.

WAYS TO NURTURE HUMAN CAPITAL

Utilizing the notion of human capital can help participants in a congregation look at their life together with a sensitive but realistic eye. Several standard church practices can be evaluated in fresh and useful ways.

The Basics: Worship

Congregations who understand and value their members' human capital usually are deliberate about stimulating its development and utilization. We can identify three common areas of a congregation's life where human capital can be nurtured. Most central, I would claim, is the worship life of the congregation. Hymns, anthems, service music, responsive readings and prayers, sharing of joys and concerns, scripture readings, preaching, sacramental ceremonies, and more all bear occasion to nourish worshipers spiritually. Worship that cultivates a sense of anticipation, that involves its "attendees" to actually participate, is far more likely to build up persons' faith and sense of belonging. Those charged with preparing weekly worship hold a tremendous opportunity in their hands.

Investing in Fellowship

One of the most underutilized avenues for nurturing member capital is through the congregation's fellowship contacts and activities. We have spoken already of the increasingly consumer-oriented attitude toward church in general and participating in a congregation in particular. If the apostle Paul is right about the value of spiritual gifts, one way that they will function more efficaciously is in a congregation who knows and cares about each other enough to be alert to opportunities. Unfortunately, the most common fellowship practice in many congregations is actually counterproductive: the "coffee hour" following Sunday morning worship. In virtually all the churches in which I have worshiped and served, the same persons talk with the same other persons week after week. While this certainly supports an existing network of relationships, it truncates the expansion of networks within the congregation. Visitors, new members, and less gregarious members often are left standing alone, literally.

I certainly am not advocating that friends never talk to each other at church or that every member in a congregation has to know and like every other member equally well! Even if this were logistically possible, given the human propensity toward sin, it would rarely occur. Given this understanding of human capital, however, church leaders would do well to treat any occasion where members interact as creative moments for encouraging investment in faith and the life of the congregation. Methods and practices will be diverse and need to be carefully thought through, planned, and regularly debriefed. Fellowship that enacts the beliefs and practices of weekly worship generates a highly desirable market for church members, not to mention visitors.

"Teach your people well"

Congregations with interesting and sought-out learning opportunities for adults are taking advantage of a third major way to nourish their membership's human capital. While there are some exciting exceptions, the state of "adult education" in many congregations today is pathetic. For many churches, the primary form is a "Sunday school" class consisting of members who have met together for a period of years and use the same kind of study materials quarter after quarter. This is not the group that will stir uninvolved adults to grow in their biblical knowledge, theological understanding, and devotional practice and animate them to Christian action. Neither will a simple appeal out of obligation (such as, "You should be coming to an adult study because church members should be learning more about their faith") motivate many.

One significant challenge to stimulate human capital through education is in developing a compelling and engaging reason for it—a reason that will overcome sleeping in, soccer games, Sunday vacations, and whatever other enjoyable activities that realistically and regularly present themselves to most church members. How to tackle this challenge goes beyond the scope of this chapter and the book, for it touches the nerve of the very question of why the church exists in the first place. Still, by pointing out its valuable potential, you can begin to mull over your church's educational ministry in terms of what it is doing to help your church's ministry. It is a sleeping giant to be gently, but persistently, aroused!

Expecting Results from Investment

In this section on nurturing human capital, we have touched on three ways to pay attention to the input side of the congregation's economic equation. Let us close this chapter with a note on the output side. The point of having and building up any kind of capital is to do something worthwhile, although somewhat risky, with it, expecting that it pays off. In the church, we call that risk "ministry" and the payoff "blessing." I use neither one of these terms here lightly or glibly. One of the paradigm shifts that seems to be offering itself to the future church is away from a passive, chaplaincy model of congregation toward an active, participatory model. Postmodern life is an almost endless array of choices, many of them appealing to immediate gratification. Why should anyone invest themselves in a congregation?

East View Church lost its pastor, who had resigned to take another position. Rev. Barr had been a popular pastor and had worked hard to help the church grow. On the day of his announcement in worship, some of the younger, newer members were teary, but the longtime members took it in stride. "We'll miss him, but we wish him well!" they said to each other. Jane was also a longtime member, but she had become active only after returning home from college, about the time that Rev. Barr had begun working at the church. She deeply appreciated his ministry, but she was realistic enough to prepare herself to move ahead with another pastor.

During the months until East View got its new pastor, Jane stayed busy with church activities—even busier than before. Already a member of the church board, Jane helped out with youth activities and Sunday school and planned fellowship events to keep church members connected to each other. But Jane began to feel some concern for the church when Sunday attendance started dropping, when communication was breaking down on the board, when activities and events were being run by the same overcommitted members, when she realized that her closest church friends were feeling the same way as she was. Jane shared some of her concern with a few other board members and at a board meeting. Their responses frustrated her: they did not seem to take her seriously, or to understand the situation in the same way.

Finally, Jane resigned her position on East View's church board. She was not looking forward to Sunday worship anymore; several of her church friends had stopped attending or participating in activities; she felt that in good conscience she could not continue as an elected leader. In the discussion that ensued over the motion to accept her resignation, board members expressed their own feelings. All of them were sorry to see her go but, no, not all of them interpreted the situation at church the way that she did. Several of the older board members had been active at East View for thirty years and more. They felt that Jane was not sticking to it, that she was impatient with the church during this interim time when things were less stable. They had seen several pastors come and go over the years, but the church is not the ministers, they said—it is the people. "We'll get through this time, too," they said, "and we'll survive."

The East View experience lifts up the matter for congregations of how human capital is invested. If we can put aside the question of whose assessment at East View was "right" or "wrong," we can see how the board members perceived investments in the church differently. For Jane, her investment seems to have been riding significantly on expecting certain kinds of results during the interim period. Of her own admission, she had not been active at East View until moving back home about the time that the previous new pastor arrived. During his tenure, Jane had become highly motivated to give much of her time and energy to the church. Apparently she was looking for a certain kind of result during the interim period. These results were not forthcoming, as she expected them. Her human capital felt spent.

On the other hand, for the longtime board members, their human capital was not invested nearly as much in the results of this particular interim period. These older members were able to draw upon positive memories of earlier days at East View to help them through the extra work and disappointments. Those positive memories pointed to invested capital from years gone by, that had paid off for them already. From their vantage point, they had invested in East View for the long haul; it would have taken a significant sense of futility before they would have curtailed their church activity.

CONCLUSION

Christians believe that life in faith is intended to produce something of lasting value and benefit. In the Fourth Gospel, Jesus says, "I came that they may have life, and have it abundantly" (John 10:10). In other words, the church carries a message to the world that, in part, claims that God seeks to take what we are and enrich all creation through it. God not only values our human capital; God seeks to expand it and use it, so that the community of creation comes to more fully express God's purposes. To realize that each one of us mere creatures is called by the incomprehensible creator-God to join in the promise for blessing to all: can we imagine a more awesome and exciting vision for life? Just as importantly, can we imagine ways not only to declare this message, but also to embody it? When we do so, in our corners of the world, we let others know that, in spite of all their other market choices, there is one that is worth their ultimate investment.

FIVE

"But Jesus Never Talked About That!"

Congregation as Collective Capacity

SNAPSHOT: CONTENTION AND ITS AFTER-EFFECTS

On a crisp March evening, 114 members of St. Matthew's Church gathered in the social hall of their church building. Built in the 1950s, the two-story brick addition that encompassed the social hall had been attached esthetically to the congregation's impressive stone, French Gothic-style sanctuary structure, a product of the proud 1920s. It was a different kind of pride, however, that spurred many of those 114 members to show up at church that night. The regular monthly meeting of the Church Council was scheduled—a meeting that for four decades or more had averaged an attendance of around twenty voting members. On this night, those 114 church members had something more than business as usual on their minds.

Word had gotten around that certain church members were going to move that night to seek the pastor's resignation. Few members were surprised by this rumor, for dissatisfaction with the pastor's performance had been dogging St. Matthew's for many, many months. A consultation process initiated twenty months earlier at the request of the pastor, Rev. Donald Peterson, had failed to alleviate the escalating circumstances. In anticipation, the Council's newly elected chairperson, Ivan Tubingen, had directed the church custodian to set up a hundred chairs in the social hall; meeting in the Ladies' Parlor on this night was out of the question.

Because of an unchallenged interpretation of the congregation's Constitution regarding voting rights on the Council, a full seventy members of the 114 who arrived at the church that night could exercise the right of Council vote. This 114 represented about one-fourth of the church's official membership; however, when compared with the average Sunday morning worship attendance of about one hundred, this Council meeting turnout was remarkable. In fact, it probably was unprecedented in the 120-year history of St. Matthew's Church.

Indeed, the meeting that night was dominated by division over the pastor. The Rev. Peterson, anticipating opposition, directed his entire comments during the pastoral report to his own defense. He capped his remarks by drawing attention to a petition in his possession, signed by 101 members of the church who supported him. Peterson was followed by a final report from the consultation group, which basically acknowledged a stalemate in their efforts to help the church. Following this report, Larry Sharif, one of the consultation group members, moved to request Peterson's resignation within thirty days or call a congregational meeting for such a vote. For the next hour, this motion was debated, in an alternating "for" and "against" format, with the Council chairperson allowing any church member who wished to speak to do so.

When the vote was finally taken on the motion for resignation, the balloting tallied to a two-to-one defeat. Peterson would not be asked to resign. On the surface, it now appeared that the conflict was over. Yet a group of "dissidents" continued to meet on their own to discuss possible next steps. Neither they, nor Peterson's most ardent supporters, anticipated what transpired at the next Council meeting. Peterson did not show up, but instead left a letter in the Council chairperson's office box.

Tubingen's face was almost ashen as he read the letter to the nearly one hundred church members who had assembled in the sanctuary that night. In somewhat ambiguous language, Peterson wrote that he realized dissident activity had led to serious damage in the congregation and that he was willing to negotiate terms of an adjustment to his pastoral duties. Legal counsel for both parties then spent weeks trying to get the ad hoc severance committee and Peterson to agree on terms. It was not until the end of August, at a specially called congregational meeting, that a multipage agreement was presented and approved. The congregation agreed to a twelve-month deal with full pay and gradual diminishment of pastoral responsibilities.

A few weeks later, the program year began at St. Matthew's Church: weekly choir in worship, Sunday school and adult studies, youth activities and seasonal events. Attendance in most areas was down; besides a staggering six summer deaths among longtime active families, several younger families either had moved away for work or ceased their involvement at St. Matthew's. The stewardship campaign for the following year projected a 10 percent deficit budget. By the end of the first quarter of the new year, Council voted to borrow cash from its own investments, in order to meet expenses.

BEYOND THE SURFACE: POWER AND POLITICS

When congregations go through protracted, escalating conflict, there are no winners, truly none. Organizational conflict has a way of escalating to a point where group members take opposing positions or else remain neutral and face potentially negative consequences from those who are convinced that one side or another is right. St. Matthew's Church was crippled seriously by the incidents of its conflict, elements of which none of the church members had wanted to occur. In all too many situations, church conflicts drain the congregation's attention and energy away from its authentic calling as God's people.

In all too many situations as well, church conflict is treated as a phenomenon isolated within itself, without any serious consideration given to what the conflict represents. Leadership in many congregations often fails to recognize the symbolic significance of the conflict. When they do, their interpretations often are both mis-leading and damning. Such interpretations often are shaped by one of two categories—theology or psychology. In theological interpre-tations of church conflict, contenders on opposite sides of the issue tend to attribute the errant ways of the other side as failure or un-willingness to follow the will of God. However, in recent years, a more common form of church conflict interpretation has been psy-chological. Here contenders attribute the position and activity of their opponents' leader as motivated by some defect or lapse (be it temporary or permanent) of personality.

This chapter is not centered on church conflict per se, nor does it aim to assess conflict interpretation or management. Other titles have addressed this topic since the 1970s.[1] We began this chapter with a true story about a church conflict because it illustrates in a most dramatic way a broader issue that always exists in congrega-tions, whether they are fighting among themselves or not. This broader issue is politics and power.

What this chapter seeks to provide is a focus upon congrega-tional politics and power in its sociocultural context. Let us step away for a moment from questions of spiritual development or psy-chological dysfunction and look at the congregation as a collective human phenomenon through yet another lens—specifically, the way that groups order, govern, act, and inevitably immerse them-selves in political dynamics, for good or ill. In congregations, these dynamics are often treated as small chunks of ice floating in the sea, easy to negotiate around, rather than the massive icebergs that they usually represent. We are ignorant and foolhardy when we pretend on the surface that power in our churches does not need to be taken seriously! Jesus dealt with power all throughout his ministry. Congregations that are healthy and effective realize that power is a complex matter for the congregation as a whole. Leaders in such congregations are prepared—not only theologically, but also strate-gically—to guide decisions and actions based on wisdom about power's necessary presence—and its peril.

POWER: A SOCIOLOGICAL VIEW

An understanding of power as something that exists because hu-mans associate with each other, and that power itself grows out of grouping and clustering, becomes evident whenever we look at history. Rome builds an empire; Mohammed spreads a new religion; Wal-Mart and Microsoft dominate their respective markets; dark horse candidates Jimmy Carter and Bill Clinton are elected to the United States presidency. Individuals who have left their mark on the world as leaders did so because of their ability to get others to do what they themselves wanted.

Defining Power

Yet power usually occurs in situations that are far from private. Forms of persuasion are often exercised in a group, as well as between groups. Weber's classic definition of power reflects both the personal and corporate dimensions. Weber says that power is "the chances which a [person] or group of [persons] have to realise their will in a communal activity, even against the opposition of others taking part in it."[2]

Such a widely held definition of power recognizes that it can be exercised in the form of a contest or fight. Perhaps that is one reason why some people in churches find the notion of power to be unwelcome or even offensive: it seems to be antithetical to the Christian gospel of love. If, however, we agree that human existence involves conditions that lead to pursuit of human intention, we will benefit from understanding how power functions—and how, in our churches, it can function more positively.

In this chapter, then, we will not be exploring power theologically. That is, our purpose is not to propose a normative definition of church power that is informed by categories from theology or spirituality. A definition along these lines, for instance, would emphasize empowerment of believers to witness to the gospel through proclamation, good works, and the like, by the agency of the Holy Spirit (see, for instance, Luke 24:48–49; 1 Cor. 12). Rather, we seek to understand how respect for common ways that power functions can equip church people to navigate the realities of power graciously and redemptively. Sometimes a cold, hard look at the way things actually are stimulates our capacity to seek what should be.

Power as Class, Status, and Party

Power takes various forms and is exercised in various ways. Weber observed that power is dispersed on the basis of three broad types of created human conditions: those concerned with a group's economic opportunity (class); those involving the evaluation of a community's specific social style of life (status); and those intentionally organized to influence community action (party).[3] We have explored two of these types (class and status) in earlier chapters, and those discussions also pertain here. The greater a group's economic class, the more power it can wield. The higher a community's or group's status, the more influence it has. The more effective a party (political or otherwise) is, the greater the power it exercises.

These three forms of power do not necessarily coexist only among the same groups of people. Mother Teresa's power was not based at all on economic chances; it was rather a power of status, in this case derived from the recognition of her particular achievement in a socially acceptable, although unpleasant, human service. In part due to her consistent religious convictions, there were occasions when Mother Teresa could use her status to influence political decisions. Conversely, a very wealthy family will maintain very high class position, but that position does not automatically guarantee high status or significant party influence. The family's specific behavior could possibly alienate others of their "station"; their political views could be so noncommittal or unconventional as to cut them off from the expected avenues of political relationship. The phenomena that create power, class, status, and party intersect, intertwine, and diverge in sometimes dizzying ways.

Status and Congregational Power, Mirroring the Community

Just like every other human association, voluntary or involuntary, congregations have a strong tendency to regard certain individuals and groups more highly than others. Recognition of such a common reality does not justify any particular ways that status gets used; it simply describes the reality as it is. Persons whose secular, community status is high are likely to be held in similar esteem by the congregation; conversely, those who are otherwise regarded as less important to society likely will be considered the same in a church, especially if that church aspires to attract or be associated with a higher status person or group. Differential treatment of individuals has a long history in congregations. The New Testament epistle of James resoundingly disapproves of the church that pays plenty of attention to the wealthy visitor but hardly gives the poor visitor a notice (James 2:1–7)! Such a biblical "precedent" highlights the tension that congregations face, if they seek to overcome the natural human tendency to follow society's status values.

Class and Power among Churches

Both societies and the churches in them, therefore, pay attention to the effects of economic dynamics. It should not surprise us, then, to observe how these dynamics lead to differing "life chances" (potential opportunities) for various churches and their church members. Any particular church's life chances will help to shape the ways in which its members perceive—and seek to utilize—power. For instance, many congregations consist of members whose economic class is very similar. Let us use a common three-part division of society to explore these distinctions.

Congregations of lower-class persons in economically marginal areas typically generate little power outside of their own church life. They often concentrate upon spiritual growth and faithfulness and upon encouraging youth and young adults to "better themselves" through clean living and education.[4] Pastors in such congregations are often charismatic and the locus of power. Poor churches usually have few resources by which power could be developed for improving local living conditions and opportunities.

Congregations representing middle-class communities usually generate quite a bit of power, focused both within their own life and within their surroundings. Experience with much wider educational and vocational opportunities leads many middle-class church members to view congregational participation as a desirable avenue for their time and energy. At the same time, however, members in these churches can be dispersed between home, job, hobbies, civic groups, travel, and other discretionary activity. These outside involvements also can affect how members view appropriate ways for their church to be active in the community. The degree to which middle-class churches are involved in community support, welfare, and change depends in large part upon how clearly such involvement is made within the church's operating vision (i.e., the church's implicit view of its purpose, regardless of any written mission statement). Hosting twelve-step groups usually is a less risky church venture than joining a coalition to support a group home or a community-based organization. Middle-class congregations usually take moderate to traditional stances on matters of mission, even though their potential for using their resources for influence and change is typically much greater than they recognize or utilize.

Congregations representing upper-middle-class and upper-class communities often face an implicit struggle, between the gospel's claim for compassion flowing from faithfulness and their world's claim to maintain control of things as they are. This is an issue that faces many middle-class churches as well, but it is seen among affluent churches in greater relief. There is a tendency to use money as the primary means of power, whether to support or deny a building project, endow an arts program, hire new staff for children's ministry, or maintain a benefactor role with particular mission projects. Of course, there are many mission projects that depend upon the generosity of churches to provide their services. This kind of giving should not be viewed as bad in itself! There is a temptation in wealthier churches, however, for power to be orchestrated rather than negotiated.

These generalizations about class, church, and power are not to be taken as iron rules; they are, however, tendencies that emerge because of the complex realities of life that churches can hardly avoid. Economic position is, for many of us, an uncomfortable topic. It is reinforced by American society's myth of rugged individualism, that anyone can achieve success and comfort if they just try hard enough. The historic impact of free market capitalism is part of the backdrop for the stage upon which all our congregations speak their lines. If our churches try to avoid or ignore the ties between economic position and power, they lose a significant edge on gospel witness.

NEGOTIATING CLASS AND POWER IN CHURCHES

One pastor of a large congregation in a comfortable community had established an unwritten policy for supporting the church's annual operating budget. He did not allow any family or member to contribute a sum in any one year of more than 2 percent of the church's budget. In this way, no member or family could use their financial support as significant leverage for church decisions. This policy was the pastor's way of minimizing the concentration of power in the congregation.

Another congregation for years had attracted the brightest and best in town to join. So highly regarded had this congregation been, it was said that you had to join it if you wanted to be eligible for the town's country club. But those days were passing; this congregation had been declining numerically for a number of years and was having a difficult time meeting its budget. The pastor had begun his ministry with the church before the decline began and knew that most members wanted the programs supported by the budget to be maintained as they were. The story is told of this pastor that, in December, he would call a few nominal members of the church who were company executives. Having calculated the year-end deficit, the pastor would divide that amount by the number of executives and invite them to make a year-end donation. This practice kept the church solvent for some years.

These two vignettes express in different ways how the interaction in churches between class and power can be negotiated. Both of these stories reflect "behind-the-scenes" pastoral practices. As we know, though, the influence of economic factors in a congregation is not always behind closed doors. Sometimes it enters the church's public arena; when it does, it represents issues larger than the one being contested.

Bavarian Church was founded some years back in a new, modest, but comfortable housing development in town. Originally a church that drew almost all of its membership from the development, Bavarian Church began to see its immediate surroundings change. Older members and residents were moving away or dying; the people buying the houses in the now-established area were younger, sometimes single, sometimes married, sometimes with young children. The church's physical plant was limited in space and could not expand on the lot. Yet a core of members, many of them younger and newer to Bavarian Church, wanted to be intentional about repositioning the church with its changing neighborhood.

An unexpected opportunity to prepare for such a repositioning presented itself when the owner of the house next door to the church building died. The house was now for sale. The pastor, young and fairly new with the congregation, saw the potential in this property and structure for expanding church programs and neighborhood outreach. So did some of the members. Financing would not be a major issue, since memorial funds could provide a large down payment. Any decision by the church to purchase this property would have to go before a vote of the congregation. The question was, would there be enough votes for purchase?

Opposition to the plan did surface. A few of the Bavarian Church's charter members still lived near and worshiped at the church. They were reluctant to spend funds that the church had saved. At the congregational meeting, some of them used this rationale to speak against the purchase. When the vote was taken, however, a large majority favored the action and passed the motion to purchase the property. Those who lost the vote, even though they would rather have had a different outcome, harbored no hard feelings.

More was at stake in the Bavarian vote than simply whether or not to take on a debt for additional property. Here was a congregation that literally was passing from one generation to another. In truth, every congregation must do this, if it is to survive. Today's changing times almost foist new circumstances on the coming generation, circumstances that often are unfamiliar and threatening to the established generation. The charter members of Bavarian Church could have mounted a campaign to block the property purchase; they just might have been able to elicit enough power to succeed. Perhaps, instead, they realized that it was not worth it. They might have been aware that the mood of the church was changing, beginning to look ahead, just like they looked ahead as young couples decades earlier, purchasing their first homes and building a church for their part of town.

Seen in this way, the resigned acceptance of the "yes" vote by longtime Bavarian members represents a willingness to allow something else that they valued highly have its way. They believed that power operates in the will of the community of faith, rather than in one group or clique. Thus they could live with a decision that they did not approve, because they chose to be part of that community.

POWER AND AUTHORITY

Class, status, and party also help us understand why power can be distinguished from the concepts of authority and role. Authority is a concept that identifies how communities establish formal relationships for delegating the right to decide, evaluate, and pass judgment on the group's activity, whether individual or corporate. This concept tends to be expressed in formal ways. Authority creates roles for certain designated positions in the community. Persons who, depending upon the community's form of governance, are deemed qualified to exercise the authority, then, are the ones who (ideally) fill these roles.

The positions of mayor and police chief impart to the office-bearers the authority—due to the official role—to act on behalf of the good of the municipality in particular ways. However, the question of whether a mayor or police chief has developed the power to effect certain decisions is sometimes distinct from whether or not that person holds the office. In other words, authority and power are not by definition identical.

Three Forms of Authority

Yet authority and power do maintain a close relationship. Weber claimed[5] that history reveals three basic forms of authority; with each form, the dynamics of power tend to be different. One of these forms arises through the focused, high-energy efforts of a person seeking to start a movement. Many religious movements begin with such *charismatic* authority. This kind of person articulates a high vision and calls people to pursue it, demanding considerable commitment. Charismatic authority is thus largely unstructured and often resides in one figure for life. Jesus, Buddha, George Fox, and Mohandas Gandhi all acquired and exercised charismatic authority.

A second ancient form of authority is called *traditional*, characterized by a stable society in which the right to decide passes through clear lines of inheritance. Traditional authority is clearly the most common form in history, as societies and cultures depended upon custom to create order, security, and transmission of practices. In many cases, the authority is most easily identified by ties of family or clan. Because of their longevity and strength, many Asian societies continue to depend in certain ways upon traditional authority; so also in Africa and the South Pacific.

A third form of authority is one that has become more prominent in the modern period. Although evidence of *bureaucratic* authority can be found in classical China, the features by which we identify this form became almost blatantly obvious throughout the twentieth century. Bureaucracy functions on the basis of rules and regulations, overseen by persons in specific roles who are appointed supposedly because of their specialized training and expertise. Its overall purpose is to process its responsibilities as efficiently as possible, by means of its ordered system of operation. Modern government of all kinds is bureaucratic, sometimes incredibly so—often aggravatingly so, as it seems often to undermine its own goals and tasks.

Yet we know that there is power in bureaucracy, which is one reason that we can feel so aggravated by it. Bureaucracy can drive us crazy, because—even when the employee or official is "just doing my job"—we can experience impersonal and slow treatment. Thus, although a customer or citizen might perceive the bureaucratic power as negative, it is power nonetheless—the power to grant, deny, or alter someone's request. Outsiders to a stable society can experience this same kind of frustration with a traditional society. Westerners who travel in traditional Islamic countries, for instance, might discover that violations of certain social and cultural prohibitions are not treated lightly. The power driving this authority is in the customs, not in what we might consider to be the "enlightened" view of basic human rights.

Tradition, Bureaucracy and Charisma in Tension

Weber's three classic types of authority can help to reveal how a congregation's decision-making processes will run into struggles over power. Rural Maple Grove Church was situated in a depressed area where young families moved in and out, looking for the satisfaction of the simple life. All the old-timers were related or intermarried and were about the only ones left whose financial circumstances did not hinge on the area's current economic conditions. Maple Grove Church membership had persisted at about ninety-five, two-thirds of which was over the age of sixty-five. Its pastors never stayed long, and they tended to be close to either seminary graduation or retirement.

One of their young pastors arrived in town ready to make a difference. After a few months, Rev. Perry began a new adult study, to attract members who did not attend the current study that used very traditional lessons. As the months went by, this eager pastor also introduced more new ideas—a music book supplement for the sanctuary, a policy on children in worship, youth liturgists, summer day trips for children, and so on. All of these proposals were either reported to, or voted upon by, Maple Grove's board. At many of these monthly meetings, appeals to all three forms of authority could be observed.

Early in his tenure, Rev. Perry concluded that no decision at the Maple Grove Church could be made without the tacit approval of four particular members, three men and one woman. All but one had roots in the area that went back many decades. Three of the four managed to hold the same offices with the church board as fully as church bylaws permitted. The authority of roles that were officially sanctioned strengthened their power. When Rev. Perry presented one of his new ideas, it already had been discussed at one of the board committees. The bureaucratic aspect of their congregation's authority was being respected and used. Perry's own explanation of the idea was couched in the kind of visionary language that a charismatic leader relishes. Newer members of the board usually favored the new ideas; the four most powerful members usually were very guarded. Their comments about the new ideas often reflected a concern not to abandon traditional practices, the ones with which they were most familiar and to which they were most committed. Eventually, it became clear to Rev. Perry that the power of traditional authority among Maple Grove Church was stronger than the appeal of charisma.

Power in the Voluntary Association

Maple Grove and Rev. Perry illustrate how each of Weber's three historical forms of authority generates different ways in which power emerges and functions. To his list, we can add a fourth form, the voluntary association, discussed in chapter 2. There we noted[6] the gradual emergence of formal fraternizations, made possible as governments and societies began to tolerate associations beyond their direct control. Over many centuries, experience with voluntary associations eventually led to forms of government (democracy) and economics (free market) that are very familiar today. As forms of maintaining state order and doing business changed, so did the nature of the power that was generated. The monolithic structures that tended to dominate history until fairly recently have given way now, in many countries, to a pluralistic situation. Much of the pluralism derives from the presence of voluntary associations—economic, political, social, and cultural—which garner their own respective powers. These powers fluctuate and shift as the particular interests of the associations must interact and negotiate with one another.

In other words, the kind of power that is present and available in postmodern society is much more complex than it used to be. People have gone to prison and wars have been waged to promote the kinds of freedoms that stimulate voluntary associational power. Historically, too, this development has involved religion heavily. New institutional forms of religion, especially in the West, became possible in part because the concept of voluntary association had become more than just an interesting proposition.

GOVERNANCE AND POWER

Differences in power between empires, feudal states, monarchies, and democracies are evident in the study of history. Yet probably the most significant power shift occurred when governments were created and based upon the citizens' right to elect their officials. Forms of democracy are much more prevalent at the end of the twentieth century than they were at its beginning.

Democracy: Promise and Peril

Guaranteeing citizens the right to associate in parties for the purpose of influencing government has been a major historical achievement. This kind of citizen participation in human experience is relatively new. At the same time, we also realize that even the power possible in democracy can be manipulated and abused. Election campaigns regularly include charges that one candidate has an unfair advantage, because of a larger treasury. Jokes are still made in Chicago about ballot-box stuffing using names of deceased residents. Bribery investigations of elected officials at all levels of American government are not uncommon. Democracy should not be worshiped because it is a panacea to power abuse, but because the right to participate in, and influence the life and activity of, the state is given to its citizens.

Religious Governance: Polity and Power.

Religious institutions in the West have developed three basic forms of governance. The most prominent form for centuries was the episcopal form, from the Greek word ἐπίσκοπος (epískopos), or "overseer," usually translated as "bishop." The Roman and Anglican Churches use this form, in which authority is vested through a hierarchical system of ordained and consecrated clergy. A second form is called presbyterial, from the Greek πρεσβύτερος (presbúteros), meaning "elder" or an older person with wisdom. Elders, sometimes both lay and ordained, are constituted as the primary form of authority for the local churches, but they also gather in larger geographical groupings to oversee business and mission activity. A third form of church polity is known as *congregational*. Here, the primary authority is vested in the congregation itself; churchwide votes on many matters are possible and likely. In its heritage, the congregational form of polity has championed the right of every church member for both voice and vote in the congregation's business.

Each one of these three forms of church polity has seated its notion of authority in differing ways. Hence, the roles established for exercising authority will be different: in episcopal, with bishops; in presbyterial, with elders; in congregational, with the church members as a body. Yet the question of power, as we already have seen, does not necessarily follow along official lines of authority and role. So also it is with church governance. The ability of church persons or groups to have their way in the church is not dictated by their formal relation to authority. The exercise of power is not limited to the avenues along which we intend it to travel.

Imitation: The Sincerest Form of . . .

This observation about the practical function of power is even more complex when we recognize how denominations that embrace all three of these polities have become very similar to each other in their national structures.[7] Complex organization, specialized division of certain jobs, drive for efficiency, and the like have moved many denominations from perhaps a more traditional form of authority to a more bureaucratic form. How does the "average person in the pew," let alone the ordained members of the denomination, make sense out of the power dynamics here? Can the bishop still get what the bishop wants? We hear a similar question from the other end of the continuum: if the local church is autonomous, why does it have to file papers with a national office and work with an outside committee when it wants to call a new pastor or borrow money for renovations?

Church Governance and the Power of Voluntary Association

Differences in denominational polity do indeed influence the ways that power can function at the level of the congregation. Episcopal and presbyterial polity has roots in Europe predating the emergence of the voluntary association as a viable institution. The authority of both bishops and the presbytery/classis operates as a check against the powers of local church authority. By contrast, congregationalism in its pure form neither develops nor seeks such "outside authority." It is voluntary association writ large. What is important to recognize about these three polities is that all three create varying ways in which power can be used and abused.

In episcopal polity, for instance, parishioners traditionally have had little or no authority in the ongoing life of the congregation. Here the overseer or bishop maintains a role that, in modern and postmodern North America at least, is sometimes questioned by parishioners and even priests and pastors. Thus, as episcopal polities make room for increased lay participation, this shift of authority creates changes in potential power dynamics. Furthermore, contests of power within a parish can continue only so long before the overseer's office becomes apprised of the situation. At that point, the parish finds out the parameters of its own authority and power.

Presbyterial polities involve a form of representative democracy at all levels, one in which authority is often interrelated from the local congregation to national agencies. This can sometimes confuse church members who are unaware of the authority relationships and the limits that go along with them. The power that develops within this web of authority will be even more mystifying to the congregation. Sometimes "going through the channels" is an unsatisfactory experience to a church member who is trying to get something done for the congregation. Any kind of pastoral change, for instance, is not a simple matter in this polity; the regional body beyond the local church makes the final approval for whatever action the congregation requests.

Because churches with congregational polity have few ties binding them beyond their local existence, their potential for power struggles turning severe tends to be greater than those for the other two polities. Here the right of voluntary association takes on its most exciting and most dramatic form. The issue is not, however, whether these churches spawn or attract individuals who love to have power! Rather, it is whether congregationally run churches maintain the resources within themselves to manage contests of power effectively. In congregational denominations such as the

United Church of Christ, covenantal relationships at regional levels do offer some avenues for balancing local authority, but these are limited compared with a presbytery or diocese.

Special Cases: Gender and Race

Because both gender and race historically have been basic categories for ascribed status (see chapter 2), many of our congregations inherit patterns of status that discriminate against women and ethnic minorities. These patterns of discrimination should be, and now are, the subject of both empirical study and theological analysis. By limiting our present purpose to the power features of status, we are suspending—but certainly not eliminating!—the question of the role of gender and race in congregational status. As a matter of policy, a number of denominations since the 1960s have been more intentional about incorporating women and other underrepresented groups in their staffing.

However, these deliberate efforts at national and regional levels to counteract wider social practices have not translated into increased racial integration among congregations. Recent history continues to serve as a painful, tragic reminder of how ignorance, fear, and hatred regarding gender and race can generate tremendous negative power. Many congregations, on the other hand, have achieved greater parity in electing women to offices traditionally reserved for men. Here is one sign that the power of traditional status perhaps is beginning to erode.

Eligibility for Office

Status also affects political decisions within the congregation. Besides creating informal networks of communication, status also influences customs concerning who is eligible for what kinds of offices and positions. In more than one Presbyterian church that I know, for instance, the election of officers has followed unwritten rules, especially regarding the sequence of office. Deacons who lead the congregation in ministries of service are the church board to which new members are usually elected first. If they are deemed to have performed their deacon duties appropriately, they then become "eligible" to be nominated for elder. The office of elder has a higher status, because elders serve on the Session, the Presbyterian congregation's governing body, where all major decisions are made. Thus, in these particular congregations, every elder also has been ordained a deacon; but not every deacon automatically becomes an elder. Congregations with other polities can and often create their own unwritten rules about office and status, with similar effect.

Authority and its Limits

Today's congregations are more likely to encourage wider participation and decision-making, through establishing committees staffed by members elected to serve on them. This is one recent development in organizational structure that, in this case, helps to disperse authority. Sometimes it is encouraged or mandated by changes in the congregation's denominational arrangement or policies.

Besides their committees and boards, congregations vest different aspects of authority in various other positions, such as staff members—the pastor, associate pastor, secretary, youth leader, custodian, for example. Nowadays, this authority is usually specified through a job description. When the influence of any person in any position with the congregation moves beyond the formal understanding of that position's parameters, the dynamic has crossed that sometimes nebulous boundary from authority to power. For authority carries formal sanction; power, on the other hand, is not necessarily contained by any formal designations.

ST. MATTHEW'S CHURCH: A STUDY IN POWER

The story of St. Matthew's Church depicts, among other things, a study in power. Let us use the concepts that we have discussed in this chapter as a way to understand the conflict there as a contest of power. Power certainly is not exercised only in situations of conflict, but conflict does help to point out how power is so much a part of a congregation's life.

There is no question that the meeting at St. Matthew's that first night was about power. It had become evident that one party in the congregation had prepared to realize their will . . . even against opposition from other church members. The main question that night seemed to be, "Who is going to win?" The parties in this contest can be distinguished in three ways. First, the one that generated the interest and high turnout in that particular meeting were antipastor; they had equipped themselves for that night, to seek his resignation. Perhaps it is worth noting that these antipastor members tended to be ones who had joined the congregation within the last decade and had been active in programs and on committees. Second, there were members who were propastor; they tended to be older, longtime members who were not as active as they once had been and appreciated specific things that the pastor had done for them. Third and less conspicuous were those members who were marginally involved and supported the pastor because they had no particular reason for wanting him to leave.

The political dynamics of St. Matthew's contest were framed that night in large part by two conceptual features that the participants probably took for granted but were ready to use to their advantage. These two features are (1) the description of their church as a voluntary association, with (2) congregational polity. This congregation's history book bears ample testimony to the strength of its voluntary nature. It had been established in a Christian tradition that had no history of state church status in Europe but instead was born out of the American experience. Furthermore, St. Matthew's tradition was free in terms of governance. Because there was no other religious layer or structure to which the congregation owed allegiance, any decisions—including conflictual ones—were treated locally, in house. No bishop or classis could step in to impose other processes or decisions upon this congregation. There were areas in its life where it was not even clear which authority rested in the Church Council and which were in the congregation overall. In a real sense, St. Matthew's was on its own.

Although the movement of that dramatic meeting climaxed in a formal vote, all three forms of authority left their mark on the evening's proceedings. Its bureaucratic form took on the representative democratic style established decades ago by the church's constitution. Historically, bureaucracies have been anything but democratic! However, St. Matthew's Church illustrates a widely dispersed trend in American voluntary associations, in which the organization's authority is spread out among boards, committees, positions, and voting members. One reason for the high turnout at this particular Council was curiosity and concern for its outcome; the other reason was to exercise constitutionally defined structures and voting rights to gain as much advantage for the respective positions as possible. Although their respective areas of responsibility were different, members of the board of trustees carried votes of equal weight to the music and education departments. At the level of bureaucratic authority, no one in St. Matthew's contest over the pastor had an edge.

At the level of traditional authority, on the other hand, an advantage probably revealed itself through the vote. Although St. Matthew's constitution circumscribed the formal process, the ability of long-standing relationships and influences within St. Matthew's membership to shape the vote cannot be ignored. As indicated earlier, a post-vote "straw poll" showed that most of those who voted against the pastor were newer members, ten years or less. Their two-to-one defeat by mostly longtime members reminds us of our discussion in chapter 3, the power of a community's culture. Longtime members usually bear the dominant views, customs, and norms of the congregation. Barring a shared sense that this culture has been violated in some way, longtime members will usually support the office of pastor and the one who holds it. Such an attitude is informal—that is, it is not voted on; it operates by association and persuasion, and sometimes even in the face of fact.

Where does charismatic authority play a part in the story of St. Matthew's? In an indirect way, it was conspicuous because of its absence. St. Matthew's Church had been seeking a pastor who could lead them back to strength. Its attendance, Sunday school, and membership figures had been dropping for many years, in spite of certain efforts to turn things around. After a pastoral retirement, the congregation's search committee was looking for new creativity and energy. They wanted to find someone whose track record and style would help draw greater numbers of new members into St. Matthew's again. They sought to stabilize their church's financial condition. They were confident that they had found these qualities in Rev. Peterson.

Those members who sought to have Rev. Peterson resign did not argue that St. Matthew's Church needed a dynamic pastor. They had simply come to the conclusion that Rev. Peterson was not the one. His use of time focused on crisis ministry rather than strategic planning for the congregation. His sermons, detractors claimed, became defensive rather than inviting. A number of members who worked closely with him complained that Peterson had a hard time letting church members offer ideas or develop a program. The party who brought the vote for resignation to the Church Council meeting that night had discussed all these concerns in detail. They had concluded that the pastoral charisma that the church needed at that time was not manifest in their present pastor.

Hence, when these three forms of authority met each other that night, something had to give. What Rev. Peterson and his supporters perhaps did not anticipate was that the vote itself was not the only way that power could be exercised. While the motion to request the pastor's resignation was defeated two to one, the contest was not over. Those who felt it was best for the pastor to leave instituted another way to exercise power, this one financial. They prepared a statement to be read at the next Council meeting, indicating their commitment to continued participation in church activities and responsibilities to elected positions. However, all who signed the statement also were pledging to withhold their financial pledges until a resolution to the pastoral question was reached. That statement was never presented, because—as we already have seen—Peterson submitted a letter to the Council himself, which triggered a negotiation process for his eventual departure. It was a move that took everyone by surprise, including members who wanted Peterson to stay.

It is not as clear in the story of St. Matthew's vote over the pastor in what ways economic class and social status affected the contest. Actually, the congregation had been losing ground, in both respects, for quite awhile. Three generations earlier, St. Matthew's status in town had been very high. By then already well-established, it had instituted the town's first newspaper, operated a large Sunday school for neighborhood children and youth, begun the first Boy Scout troop in town, spawned an annual community flower show, run a summer youth camping program, and constructed a beautiful stone sanctuary. St. Matthew's Church was a leading player in its community's life. During this same era, the congregation's economic class was also enviable. Surrounding its impressive facilities were large, attractive houses on tree-lined streets. A number of area business executives were known to be St. Matthew's members. Mission giving was a significant part of their annual budget.

St. Matthew's Church wore its upper-middle-class status proudly through four decades. However, demographic changes after World War II gradually reduced the number of potential new members. The town's thirteen churches in 1920 numbered thirty in the

1960s. Net membership had dropped almost two-thirds by the time that Rev. Peterson arrived. St. Matthew's visibility in town was much lower then than it had been; other congregations had become "the place to be." When St. Matthew's contended over its pastor, the only residents in town who seemed to notice were a few old-timers who derived some pleasure in hearing of the once-grand congregation's troubles.

CASE SUMMARY

St. Matthew's Church was the scene of a significant contest over who was in control of the pastoral office. This contest called into play the congregation's authority structures, as they were defined by the church bylaws and consequent role definitions. The congregation's "dissident" members demonstrated a creative approach to developing power, noteworthy in part because of what it did not do. Rather than attempt to win votes through a character assassination of the pastor (which probably would have escalated the tension ever more), the dissidents instead focused upon performance in the pastoral role. They tried to emphasize their view that Rev. Peterson did not have all the pastoral skills that their congregation needed. For his part, Peterson was able to use his role as pastor to garner interest primarily from traditional members in retaining him. The eventual resolution of Peterson's tenure lifts up an important insight for congregations—that formal votes usually cannot contain or dismiss opposing forces. The power of voluntary church members to choose another church and the freedom of members to create power in new and unexpected ways should not be underestimated.

LESSONS FOR LEADING

Reviewing St. Matthew's story not only illustrates concepts of power that have been mentioned already; it also suggests some other features of power that are significant. For one, power is not bad or good in itself: it is what it is, power. To argue that St. Matthew's dissident members were wrong (or even unchristian) to organize themselves, so that their concerns would be treated seriously, would be naïve. The question is not, "Is there power in a church?" but "How is it used?"

These so-called dissidents demonstrated, secondly, that power does not rest forever in one place: it can and does move, depending on circumstances. This insight perhaps should be an obvious one, but church people sometimes forget it. Clarence Stone, a scholar of the American urban scene, makes the point as he reviews the dynamics of Atlanta governance since World War II. Large cities, Stone argues, get things done through "informal arrangements" that develop between both the public and private sectors. As change happens, conflict must be faced with adaptation.[8] Both political and economic interests play out in the "regime politics" of cities.[9] Working together to negotiate these interests presses all parties to cooperate, thus leading to a give-and-take dynamic that depends upon relationships.[10] Consequently, power itself is fluid;[11] it never stays the same or in one place all the time. This fluidity also becomes evident in congregations.

A third factor about power to highlight at this point in the chapter is that power can be creative. Consider, for example, Mohandas Gandhi's twenty years of efforts to help India gain its independence from Britain. It was a complex set of political, social, and economic dynamics within which Gandhi had to operate. His hunger strikes and wildly reverent popularity with the masses of untouchables functioned as two of his more creative means of developing and exercising power. In a much less dramatic fashion, St. Matthew's dissident members worked together to use the congregation's governance process as its platform for presenting its concerns about their pastor's performance. Part of their creativity rested in a tactic that was unexpected. Yes, they did request that the pastor resign, but they did so without attacking him personally. Rather, they distinguished between Peterson as a conscientious person and his performance as their pastor. This tactic helped to maintain attention on their central concern and reduce inflammatory side conflicts.

Finally, power can be discretionary. Just because a person or group perceives themselves as powerful does not mean that the power has to be used "against" others. St. Matthew's dissidents did create power for themselves, but they sought to employ it judiciously. Their deliberate effort points to the kind of use of power that Eric Law encourages in his teaching and writing. In his first book,[12] Law borrows from Geert Hofstede's theory of "power distance"[13] to contrast differences between ethnic groups in terms of tendencies for perceiving power. Having been born in Hong Kong and then raised from his teen years in the United States, Law's interest in culture and power grow out of his own personal experience. He notes differences in cultural assumptions between the dominant, white-oriented American middle class and many communities of color. Whereas white society tends to encourage individual self-assertion based upon assumptions of equality, people of color tend to be acculturated toward a view that individuals do not have power. These generalizations paint broad strokes, Law admits, but they help nonetheless to point to general tendencies and expectations in wider American society.[14] People who live in the United States tend to sense that race and culture influence the location of and capacity for power.

As a theory, these purported differentials in perceptions of power attempt to describe human patterns of behavior that are observable. In Law's hands, however, they also offer to Christians a theological framework for overcoming the injustices that the differentials usually perpetuate. As I mentioned just previously, power is a commodity that can be discretionary. What happens in a Christian, multicultural context when those perceived with more power try to take seriously sharing it? Law's answer to this question comes in the form of a notion that he calls "the cycle of Gospel living."[15] People whose race and culture locates them consistently in opportunities for power enter the cycle by giving power to those who typically do not have it. As symbolized in the resurrection, usually people of color are empowered and strengthened. For whites, on the other hand, the cycle calls for them first to empty themselves as Jesus did in his crucifixion.

Giving power away calls for deliberate discretion. Yet, as Law emphasizes,[16] power must not remain static: it needs to shift from group to group, in order to fulfill its gospel purpose for justice. Hoarding power creates polarities between privilege and oppression. For Christians seeking to follow the gospel, learning to share power is at the heart of living the faith.

CONCLUSION

Jesus did talk about power! He spoke against religious leaders who misled the people by following rules without spirit (Matt. 23:13–36). He released persons from the power of evil spirits (Mark 5:1–20). He said that those who live by the sword die by it (Matt. 26:52). He bemoaned the Holy City that killed God's prophets (Luke 13:34). Jesus, and the apostle Paul after him, had a keen sense of how human structures make certain things possible and other things difficult. In a sense, Jesus' message is all about power. It is about yielding our lives to the way of God, so as to become God's partners in a grander, more blessed way of existence that shares opportunity among all God's creatures.

In this chapter, we have explored several concepts and structures of power that can help us interpret some of the complex dynamics of a congregation. In itself, power by definition is not bad; it just is. The question is how power is used and for what purposes. Church leaders can find in these concepts fresh insights for the many inevitable, necessary, and even potentially beneficial moments when power must be exercised. It is one of a congregation's ongoing challenges to recognize power, to encourage its development, and to share it for the good of the gospel vision that the church proclaims and follows.

S I X

Being "Like Other Nations"

Congregation as Complex Organization

IN COMMON WITH OTHERS

In preparing yourself for this chapter, first think in some particular ways about a congregation that you know. Take a few minutes and jot some notes about the following:

Taking Stock

- When was your congregation founded? What was the surrounding community like at that time? What is it like now? How much has changed/stayed the same? —peak

- What is the latest significant change that your congregation dealt with? How did it take place? What was the congregation's response?

- What words and phrases best describe the way that your congregation looks and acts most of the time? Be sure to include characteristics of your church that are both complimentary and not so complimentary.

- What shape does your congregation's organizational life take? How elaborate is its structure? What has led to this current setup?
- How is your church different from other organizations in your community? How is it similar?

After reading this chapter, I encourage you to reflect on your notes. For right now, we are getting ready to enter another world that is opened up to us through one of the social sciences. It is a world that, to many church members, feels too wooden to have anything to say about congregations. However, if we look closer, we begin to realize how much our churches have in common with other organizations of today. For in the last few generations, the experience of many—if not most—congregations has taken on features that feel quite familiar outside of church, too. In modern societies, churches look and behave like many other organizations, organizations that can and do have very different purposes.

Ancient Precedent

A religious group looking and even behaving like other groups around it is not new to our present era. After the Israelites had entered the promised land and received their allotments, they were ruled for a period of time by "judges." Judges were individuals chosen by God to provide leadership in crisis and to adjudicate community disputes. Their selection was verified within the community by some mighty act that the people recognized as inspired by God—often through leading a successful battle against the intruding Canaanites. Before too long, however, the Israelites were not satisfied having judges as rulers. Looking around the vicinity of their country, they were well aware that the other peoples maintained their own monarchies, with the trappings of power, majesty, and glamor. The Israelites must have been envious. They hounded the elderly and righteous judge Samuel to give them a king. Israel wanted to "be like other nations" (1 Sam. 8:1–9).

Ancient Israel got what it asked for—and more! Along with the monarchy came conscription and taxes, two characteristics of a movement that becomes institutionalized (see chapter 2). One of the ways that this insight from the Scriptures speaks today is in reminding churches about that fascinating tension they face with the world around them. This tension is about imitating what other communities do, while still taking advantage of things that work well. This tension is even more salient today, since one of the most significant legacies of the twentieth century has been so taken for granted.

A Proliferating Phenomenon

While it is clear that people have been organizing themselves for a vast array of tasks since recorded time, it is also clear that organizing has taken on a dimension in our time that is unparalleled. Since the generation following the Civil War, the organization of businesses and governments in the United States has multiplied dramatically.[1] Their specific form will be discussed in the following section, but it is worth noting here that the kind of organization to which we have become familiar went through its own challenges to emerge. Formal organization, with its rules, records, officers, and so forth, met resistance until changes in the law encouraged its development. One of the eventual effects of this proliferation of organizations can be seen in records of public discourse. References on the front page of *The New York Times* to individuals and to organizations reversed themselves in the century between 1876 and 1975. Whereas articles about individuals were most conspicuous on front page news in 1876, by the 1970s it was dominated by organizations.

Hence, it is indisputable that we live in a world that creates organizations. Family-owned businesses, huge corporations, international firms, governmental bodies at all levels (i.e., municipal, county, state, regional, and federal), professional associations, fan clubs, book and hobby clubs, parachurch groups, and so on, and so on: it is impossible in this era for a person influenced by Western practices to avoid contact with several of these kinds of organizations. As Max Weber argued almost a century ago,[2] one of the characteristics of organizations is that they take on a life of their own. In other words, groups that survive over long periods of time do so in part because their activities do not depend on the participation of specific individuals. Rather, the organization expects and garners others who will carry on. Throughout its long history, the witness of the Church has taken this feature closely into account. At the same time, however, some Christian thinkers have interpreted survival like this as a compromise to secular forces.[3] There is a risk, some in the Church have believed, in imitation.

Three general purposes guide the discussion in this chapter. One is to show how recent understandings of organizations apply to congregations. A second, by implication of the first, is to broaden our perspective on the role of organizations in this postmodern era of ours. A third is to suggest ways that readers can begin to use a new generation of organizational concepts to both understand and help their churches.

PERSPECTIVES ON "THE ORGANIZATION"

We begin by first getting a historical bird's-eye view of how organizations have been studied and interpreted.[4] This overview will help us appreciate how organizational theory has developed and what church people have at their disposal.

Machinelike Efficiency

The first full-fledged theory about organizations is often credited to Max Weber and can be labeled in more than one way. This theory looks at organizations primarily as entities in themselves, who set up their way of doing things in order to be as efficient as possible. Its basic characteristics include a clear division of labor, training for each position, procedures and rules, record keeping, and a hierarchy of responsibility. Terms such as rational-legal bureaucracy, scientific management, and machine have been used to describe this theory. It is the classic one that shaped organizational life during the turn of the twentieth century. Its major proponents, so to speak, were the growing number of governmental bodies in Europe and the United States, along with an even faster-growing number of capitalist ventures.

Feeling Good and Getting Along

By the 1930s, however, some organizational observers believed that the machine theory has its limits. These observers were persuaded that the organization also needs to pay attention to its people; a company's performance and prospects, they argued, are affected significantly by its employees. Out of this interest in the human dimension—spurred by some famous early experiments in social psychology—came the theory known as human relations, or more recently organizational development. These days, many companies with personnel offices use the term human resources, as a nod to this theory's emphasis upon worker morale, communication, participation in decisions, and so on.

Many large businesses, while still seeking to be as efficient (machinelike) as possible, also recognize that their employees need to feel good about what they are doing and motivated to achieve. Thus many companies today operate implicitly with strategies that derive from both of these organizational theories. In recent years, for instance, some companies have spent time and money sending their staffs to training in activities such as high ropes courses. Activities like this force the staff members to work together; they learn new things about themselves and each other; they take calculated risks and achieve some rewarding experiences; they bond with each other in new ways. From there, it is anticipated that the staff will be more trusting, energetic, creative, and productive at work. "Quality Circles" and "Total Quality Management" are on-the-job participation methods for accomplishing the same purpose. The company benefits from paying attention to the human relations side of its existence.

Interactive

In more recent years, still other organizational observers have promoted various versions of yet another theory of organizations. This theory assumes that what goes on around an organization is just as important to its existence and activity as its internal life. In other words, organizations—unlike in the other two theories—do not function as closed systems; they relate with, and are influenced by, the various elements of their environment. This notion that the organization-environment relationship is fundamental lies at the heart of open systems theories.

One of the advantages, but also challenges, of an open systems perspective on organizations is that it is so dynamic. What the organization is and does is understood in terms of its interaction with outside elements, through active, give-and-take processes, as it provides its products or services. More of what actually occurs seems to be easier to account for through open systems. The flip side of this observation is the potential ambiguity or confusion that the organizational observer can experience. Because open systems theory seeks by definition to be more comprehensive than either the classical or human relations theories, there can be moments when it is not easy to sort out all the factors involved in the organization's behavior or experience.

MORE CONCEPTS FROM OPEN SYSTEMS THEORY

Recent literature in organizational research includes various specific versions of open systems theory, but they are not necessary for our purposes here. It is sufficient to have introduced the generic version of this model. As we proceed in this section, open systems will stand as our first concept from organizational theory. Designating it in this way is technically inaccurate, since a theory consists of a set of concepts in a particular relationship with each other. Yet, since it is our orienting point for this chapter, we will allow it to stand with the rest of the concepts. We turn to them now.

Environment and Its Basic Features

Our second concept has already been introduced: environment. This is also a broad category, for it refers to anything in the context or surroundings of the organization. As implied above, environment is an integral feature of any organization. Its elements are many and varied. One way to distinguish between them is to think of those that can be easily measured (quantifiable) and those that are more elusive at first glance but nonetheless influential (qualitative). Easily measurable elements include many demographic features, such as population density, climate, geography, ethnic diversity and ratios, education and income levels, percentage of owner-occupied homes, and distance from and commute times to work. This kind of information is gathered each decade by the Census Bureau and is easily accessible.

There are other elements of environment, however, that are not so quickly discerned. Anyone who has grown up in one country or part of a country and moved to a different part has experienced this subtle but powerful phenomenon. We discussed in chapter 3 the several layers of culture; these layers carry characteristics that in large measure define the qualitative elements of environment. Local and regional habits, attitudes, beliefs, popular expressions, and so forth exist everywhere. They don't appear in tourist photographs! Yet the effect of these qualitative environmental features upon the life and possibilities of those in the area cannot be underestimated.

Variability of Environments

Environments change; they rarely stay the same for long periods of time. Factors such as population mobility, economic conditions, war, climate shifts, natural disasters, cultural revolutions, and the like can and do alter the landscape within which congregations live and move and have their being. And just as significant, environmental changes occur at widely differing ranges of speed and scope. The "fall" of the Roman Empire, for instance, took place like a long erosion that finally led to large cracks and eventual breaks in the empire's political, legal, and economic systems. In terms of speed, this so-called "fall" took decades to occur. In terms of scope, there is no question that it affected the behavior of virtually every person and institution in the West. By contrast, the personal computer revolution of the 1980s distinctly altered certain practices of businesses, schools, and many households heavily shaped by Western technology. However, it does not yet alter in a direct way the living patterns of millions of persons who live in countries where most of the population cannot afford to purchase and benefit from such technology. Rome illustrates gradual environmental change on a comprehensive scale; personal computing illustrates fairly rapid environmental change on a more distinctly limited scale.

In other words, the actual change in environments can range in predictability and appearance from monolithic to chaotic. Similarly, because the various elements of changing environments are so diverse, they can influence different kinds of organizations in different ways. Take the hypothetical comparison of a small evangelical Protestant congregation in rural Mexico and a large, well-endowed suburban congregation in the United States. Let's say that on one particular day, coincidentally, a large mud slide travels through the little church's village in Mexico, while the Dow Industrial Average on Wall Street drops twenty percent. Both events will significantly influence something in their immediate environments! At the same time, neither church will be seriously affected, at least in the short-term, by the environmental change that was closest to the other church's way of life.

Environment, then, is like the water in the fishbowl that everyone takes for granted until it starts looking different than most people expect. How people and their organizations respond to those changes tells us something about how they perceive the water and the bowl.

Churches in Open Systems: The Chicago School

Nearly a century ago, while sociology was emerging as a major discipline in the United States, a group of professors connected with the University of Chicago were studying the city and creating the "Chicago School" of sociology.[5] Based upon this early work, we can recognize now their insistence of the influence on the concept of environment. These scholars used terms like "ecology," "natural communities," "adapt," "expansion," and "sectors" to describe what they perceived to be quite predictable processes affecting populations, regional settlements, shifts, and so forth. It became evident to them that demographics, culture, traditions, immigration, and the like deeply shaped what people did in certain places and how they organized themselves. This tradition of sociological study is significant for our purposes, in more than one respect. First, as just suggested, its ecological perspective lifted up the intricate, sometimes subtle, ties between the various elements of a human community. That is, the Chicago School took environment very seriously.

Why Churches Die

Secondly, the research on city churches that flowed out of this school of research offers an implicit argument for open systems theory. Kincheloe argued that many Protestant congregations did not and could not survive when the ethnicity of their neighborhoods' populations completely changed.[6] What one people valued, sought, and did together in their communities usually was so distinct that new immigrants were not attracted to them; besides, they invariably brought their own institutions—including churches—with them. The ability of churches not to adjust to ethnic/cultural changes illustrates one facet of interrelationship and exchange that open systems theory reveals.

Kincheloe himself was a pastor who studied sociology and later taught it to seminary students after watching a struggling city congregation die under his feet. He and his students observed over the years[7] many churches that began with great hopes and strong activity gradually lose members to migration and death. As the church would wane, members tended to find fault with the pastor, with slack members, with the neighborhood's new immigrants and sometimes with their denominational agency. Its mood would swing between hope and despair, as it became nostalgic about its earlier accomplishments and its building. Sometimes, before the congregation moved, merged, or disbanded, it would try to focus its efforts on community services, especially with the children and teenagers of the immigrant families. In most cases, these efforts were frustrating and short-lived, and the church finally would discontinue its activity.

As we obviously know, not all churches are in large cities. Yet church-in-the-city studies put into most bold relief the large-scale factors that influence congregations everywhere, to some degree. When we look at congregations by beginning with their context, we become more vividly aware of the nature of the "water" in which the "fish" swim. This metaphor could be misleading here, however, since the fish in this application are not persons but congregations. If a congregation, as an organization, does take on a life of its own, then to some significant degree it relates to the water around it as a distinct entity. Such entities are not anything in general but something in particular. We would not expect, for instance, to find a Ukrainian Orthodox congregation in a town filled with German Catholic farmers and merchants.

Organization: A Definition

So far in this chapter about congregations as organizations, we have said little about the concept of organization itself. It was important for us to look first at the two previous concepts, since they provide the framework for how "organization" is defined here. Most of us probably think of an organization as something large, with a full structural chart of divisions and offices, having been in existence for many years, inhabiting impressive or interesting-looking buildings, offering products and/or services, and so forth. This picture of organization derives largely from the "machine" model of organizations that, in many respects, still dominates our thinking. However, if we think of the concept in broader terms, it will help us appreciate more fully the place of congregations in the organizational life of today's world.

In other words, organizations can be considered not only impressive corporate and governmental bodies, they also can include small, even rather transient, collective human endeavors. Along these lines, then, we will define our third concept. An "organization" is *any human activity requiring coordination and cooperation of effort from a number of persons performing roles with an expectation that the activity will be maintained over some period of time.*

This definition is intended to be broad. When your great-grand-mother's family helped to found that immigrant church on the fron-tier many decades ago, she was not expecting it to become the size of IBM. Yet, with the definition we are using here, she and her col-leagues in faith had established an organization.

As has been implied already, organizations can be and are ex-tremely diverse in size, goals, locations, requirements for member-ship, activities, resources, products and services, survivability, and the like. Still, we discover some common threads among this great diversity: the fact that people are together doing something that, to some extent, lasts over time. This is true whether it is little league, Standard Oil, a fan club, the American Library Association, a radio-controlled model airplane club, the City of New York, Ben & Jerry's Ice Cream, a gang, or your congregation. In spite of the vastly different ways that they can and do operate, organizations share the denominator of people coming together to accomplish a purpose. With this definition, many collective human ventures are "organized."

MANAGING AND ADAPTING: AN INEVITABLE TENSION[8]

A fourth concept that can be useful for understanding organizations is the notion that over time, organizations face the rhythm between two particular extremes. We touched on this idea in sociological terms in chapter 2, as we discussed movements and institutions. This same general phenomenon occurs among organizations. Rarely, if ever, do organizations that have survived a century or so begin their existence with the level of members, resources, and ac-tivities that they later enjoy. Instead, brand-new organizations tend to start small, driven by one or a few highly committed persons, fo-cused on the task in such a way that intimacy is strong; a family feeling characterizes the organization's experience. Young organiza-tions tend to be movementlike. The converse is also true: after some years to reach a level of size and activity, there is no guarantee that any organization will maintain it all indefinitely. Older organiza-tions tend to be institutional.

This double phenomenon can be stated in a way that pertains particularly to organizations. They must learn to be adept at two basic processes that are the opposite of each other: to control what they do while also being capable of adapting to changes. In order to survive and thrive, organizations must be able to both control and adapt themselves, virtually at the same time.

What members of many organizations fail to accept or realize is that neither one of these opposites can be preferred as better than the other, if the organization intends to continue and stay healthy. The high number of failed new businesses in the United States each year attests to the need to learn control; an organization in early stages cannot do everything, for its resources are limited. Conversely, organizations that control their operations to the point of prizing repetition risk being unable to make changes when circumstances warrant them.

Schwinn's Near Miss

When the Schwinn bicycle company was purchased in 1993, a new era—indeed, a new life!—began for America's most well-known name in two wheels. Schwinn had been a household name for decades, the bicycle of choice for hundreds of thousands of children—a full 25 percent of the market. By 1992, however, when it filed for bankruptcy, Schwinn's share of the bicycle market had dropped to an abysmal seven percent. In an era when mountain bikes had become standard fare on suburban streets, Schwinn's products were known as old and stodgy. It seems evident that Schwinn, founded in Chicago in 1895, had lost its flexibility.

The company that bought Schwinn spoke during the transition of a "rebirth." The company was moved to Boulder, Colorado, as a wholly owned subsidiary of a company there. The language used to describe the new owners' vision for Schwinn was laced with the word "new": a new company, new attitude, new products, "a chance of a lifetime." Now, that is flexibility talking!—a flexibility that the family-owned Schwinn company was not able to produce on its own.

In the competitive world of business, Schwinn ended up lucky. Overcontrol eventually has bad effects upon the organization's behavior and subsequently its health. Some organizational researchers[9] have elaborated upon the way in which some of this overcontrol looks. When adaptability wanes, organizations continue to focus on form and structure, as a way to maintain the semblance of being in control; hence they become increasingly interested in looking good and being well regarded. Other researchers[10] even argue that, when well-established organizations are uncertain about the future, they imitate the form and style of organizations that they consider peers within their field. Such institutional "isomorphism" does nothing, however, to improve the organization's productivity or performance. Is it true, for instance, that every corporation derives the same benefits from having a large number of high-profile persons sitting on its board? Probably not, but when "everybody who is anybody is doing it," perceived security from status is more persuasive than reason.

Church Imitation

Institutional isomorphism can become a trap into which well-meaning leaders of well-established churches can easily fall. Congregations can assume when they begin to worry about their future that maintaining clear structures and attempting to keep that machinery operating will take care of their needs. This is a particularly tempting approach, given the way that rational-legal bureaucracy has been treated in this century as a model for organizational efficiency. In fact, virtually all mainline Protestant denominations adopted this model early in this century, from the congregation on up. Moreover, I would even claim that in the mid-twentieth-century growth of denominational structures, staffing and programming beyond the local church reflects in part the rigidifying effects of organizational institutionalism. Ironically, this phenomenon occurred as its designers and participants expected it to assist, rather than to confuse, slow, or hinder, the denominations' work.

Cart or Horse?

St. Matthew's Church illustrates the dangers of organizational imitation at the congregational level. A congregation that was founded after the Civil War in a new village, the church gradually grew in numbers and activity as its village grew and eventually annexed with a nearby growing city. Twenty-five years after its founding, St. Matthew's was led by a board with a total of eight positions, representing the pastor, two elected deacons, treasurer, clerk, and three trustees. This was at a time when its membership had reached about 185 confirmed members. Another four decades later, St. Matthew's neighborhood was bustling; its membership was around seven hundred and it reached a peak of its organizational complexity. Board positions now numbered eighteen, with other church groups having a grand total of more than one hundred other elected positions (not counting group membership itself). This number of positions actually was reduced right after World War II, to sixteen and about fifty-five, at a time when the congregation membership figures had stayed fairly level.

During the boom church-going 1950s, St. Matthew's Church began to grow again, and so did its organizational size—to twenty-three board positions and more than sixty-five others. The next observation does not make logical sense, but it can be understood in light of the concept of institutional isomorphism. St. Matthew's hit its membership peak of almost a thousand members in 1965, but it lost members—almost as a barometer to the national mainline Protestant trend—every year from then on. Yet its organizational structure remained basically intact for the next three decades. In 1988, when its membership was down under five hundred and weekly worship at one hundred, board positions remained at twenty; other church group positions were actually higher than thirty years earlier—up to eighty-one. On a given Sunday, most of those attending worship sat on one of the elected boards and committees!

These figures suggest a resistance by an insecure congregation to adjust any of its structure. A closer look at St. Matthew's records seems to support this conclusion. The total number of organizations within the congregation over its lifetime was eighteen, not counting scout troops and a few elected positions with no specific committee. Sixteen of these eighteen were functioning in 1955, during its second boom period (the first was in the 1920s), while by 1988 that number was down one-third, to twelve. Perhaps most significantly, the organizational structure of St. Matthew's Church remained pretty much as it had been for decades, even though its membership was half of its peak size and—more telling—its average Sunday attendance dropped to one-third of its peak.

This look at the history of the organizational arrangement of St. Matthew's Church helps us understand more vividly the effects on congregations of institutional isomorphism. When a well-established church begins to lose ground in numbers and activity, it tends to keep things running as they always had run. As we saw above, this phenomenon is not unique to religious organizations! But it does not have to be inevitable.

Institutional isomorphism reveals in one particular way something that one of the organizational concepts frames in a broader way. When we consider the continuum that every organization faces between managing and adapting, we see that isomorphism is a form of the organization getting too controlled. By framing this concept as a continuum, we see also that the danger of a church becoming rigid is one end of a spectrum that usually occurs over a period of time. The other end of the spectrum is the danger of being too flexible, of not controlling itself enough. Either extreme hurts the congregation. However, because churches that are too flexible usually end up closing before they can get established, we tend to hear more about the older churches that have gotten "stuck in the mud."

A Giant Adapts: Sears

Whether or not you agree specifically with what they did, you cannot argue that Sears, Roebuck and Company made some changes in the early 1990s that kept it a viable business. In contrast to Schwinn, which we noted above did not make changes until it was bought out, Sears did not wait long after seeing red ink to demonstrate that it could be flexible. That must have been challenging, since for many decades Sears had been so consistent and so much a part of American life. Its then-innovative catalog became a household word, giving generations of Americans practical, reliable goods as well as the stuff that dreams are made of—especially around holiday time!

Yet quarterly profits were dropping in the early 1990s and, for the first time in almost sixty years, Sears posted a quarterly loss—a big one, of more than 1.5 billion dollars. Eighteen months later, Sears had managed three straight quarters of decent earnings, leading financial analysts to applaud the company again. What had they done to turn things around so quickly, at least financially? Probably the single most key action was to discontinue the revered catalog operation. It had been losing millions of dollars for a number of years. In a similar move, Sears got out of its dealings in real estate. All in all, the company eliminated more than fifty thousand jobs. They also instituted a new ad campaign to encourage shoppers to buy Sears clothing.

Analysts are left to dicker over whether any of Sears' particular actions during this financial crisis were the best ones to make. That is not our purpose here. Rather, we are highlighting the fact that Sears made major decisions quickly; leadership bit the bullet of change. These actions helped the company to survive and look forward again. Unlike Schwinn, Sears did not get absorbed by another company in order to survive through flexibility. Sears adapted on its own—one of the virtual necessities of any modern organization.

Congregations on the Continuum: Simplifying

Occasionally congregations realize on their own that they have to be flexible, even if it means changing their own structures. Dellwood Church found itself even smaller after a protracted difference of opinion concerning finances and pastoral performance split the congregation. With a history more than a century long, and a tradition that valued spiritual development and close fellowship, the split was painful. When the pastor in question had begun there, Sunday attendance was in the forties; after he left, it was down to twelve.

It was clear to everyone who wanted to stay that their little church might need to fold. Yet they also knew that they needed time to allow the pain of the past two years to subside, so that healing and renewal could be possible. They also realized that there simply were not enough persons to do everything that had been done before. So they decided to consolidate all their committees into only three: internal relations, mission, and operations. The majority of the members who remained with this church had joined within the last ten to fifteen years, although a few lifelong members were included. The latter had the hardest time getting used to the structural change but, for the congregation as a whole, it was a welcome and certainly more efficient decision.

Too "Loosey-Goosey"

Douglas Walrath[11] tells the story of Newton Church, which illustrates an excessive flexibility that most of us do not encounter firsthand. A denominational body had made a financial commitment to begin a new congregation in a growing suburb and had brought in an organizing pastor who seemed to have great potential. After two years, however, the presbytery staff began to realize that Mark might have had great potential, but it was not in organizing. It was not that Mark was not "gung ho" to help this new church take off.

Five years into the new venture, the question became whether Mark's approach could be salvaged.

Mark himself admitted to others that he did not want to create a church that was very structured. So this young congregation established no committees. Once a year they held a potluck and talked over what they were doing and what they might do. The glue that held everything together, when it did, was the force of Mark's personality and commitment to caring for the flock. Yet the presbytery knew that this church should have been able to grow to two hundred members in five years. Instead, it had crested at sixty-nine after the fourth year. The congregation's debt also was growing. Clearly something needed to be done. Still, after more than a year of working with a consultant, the church had only seventy-eight members; most of the original leaders were burnt out and left, including Mark. This was one new church that should have survived but did not.

Walrath's analysis of this young congregation's failure picks up the problem of excessive flexibility in more than one respect. For one thing, as we have seen, Pastor Mark intentionally pursued a style of leadership that drastically reduced the church's interest in creating appropriate structure. Emphasis instead was placed upon strong fellowship and caring for individuals; Pastor Mark believed that this was a sufficient approach to creating a healthy church. Secondly, the resultant congregational pattern, while on one level effective at personal affirmation, actually made it more difficult for the congregation to try new things. There were no clear ways to figure out what to do, how to do it, whether and how to revise something. People became worn out as decisions had to be made haphazardly and inefficiently. Third, the freewheeling style blunted the ability of the congregation to grow. So much revolved around Pastor Mark that he could serve only so many persons on his own. In a sense, there was room for just a limited number of people to become part of this church's life.

Here is the sad and painful story of a new church that should have made it but didn't. In spite of initial enthusiasm, the congregation had stayed so movement-like, so open-ended, that it collapsed in on itself. As an organization, then, congregations do not benefit from seeking one end of the control-adapt continuum or the other. Either extreme will take its toll.

When the Spirit Says "Move". . .

In chapter 2, we saw how True Spirit Church, in a dramatically changing context, adapted itself successfully by articulating a new vision. As a result, True Spirit grew significantly in numbers and programming. Unfortunately, not every congregation is poised to shift directions so quickly and effectively. What made the difference in this one case? Part of the answer lies in the fact that this church was barely fifteen years old when it made the change, and that two-thirds of its members had left already. The core who remained was committed to working together and creating something new. They were flexible when the environment forced them to be so. Otherwise, that church might have folded up after a few more years—a victim of ignoring organizational wisdom about balancing adaptability with manageability.

Tuning In

A group of leaders in a different congregation decided that they needed to be flexible in a new way. During a renewal training process, leaders of Prairie Home Church reviewed their community's demographics and saw few, if any, significant changes. Their community continued to be a fairly typical Anglo, upper-middle-class suburb. As they discussed changes in the macroculture, however (see chapter 3), the team realized that the generation following them is not very interested in church. A lot has been written about the "buster" generation, young adults born after 1964, and about the children of their generation.[12] This team concluded that their 150-member, thirty-five-year-old congregation needed to be more deliberate in reaching out to the growing number of these persons in their community.

From this book's viewpoint, it is not healthy for an organization to be either too flexible or too controlled. We should be able to easily recognize institutionalism among, say, mainstream Protestantism, because there are so few young congregations in those traditions that are risking much adaptability. Some pastors in another family of churches (such as evangelical or pentecostal) might be able to give us quite a bit of anecdotal insight about the problems of newer churches. The point is that some tension has to be maintained between the two poles. Healthy churches must maintain a working balance between the repetition of control and the freedom of adaptation. Either end of the spectrum yields unpleasant, even tragic, results.

ORGANIZATIONAL GROWTH AND DECLINE: AN OPEN SYSTEMS DEFINITION

Acknowledging the continuum of controlling and adapting—and its related concept, institutional isomorphism—points us toward another salient pair of organizational concepts. This pair is that of "growth" and "decline." In the literature, these two notions typically are tied closely to factors that can be easily measured. These would include elements such as size of workforce or membership, budget, physical facilities and their condition, profit margins, quarterly earnings, number of contributors, and so on. In these terms, a declining organization is one that is witnessing reductions in such quantifiable elements of their life. Conversely, a growing organization would be seeing these numbers increasing.

In this chapter, we offer a definition of decline that does not categorically dismiss quantifiable factors; yet it focuses the critical characteristic elsewhere. This definition of decline is tied to the organization's relationship with its environment. Here, decline is seen as the organization's inability to adapt when the environment changes or to maintain its role or niche when the environment is stable.[13] Conversely, then, a growing organization is one that does alter its behavior to respond to changes in its context, or maintains its particular activity and character when the context is constant.

The difference between these two sets of definitions reveals the different perspectives within organizational theory between closed and open systems. In a closed system, what is paramount to the organization consists of the organization's own activities. In an open system, what is paramount to the organization consists of the sometimes subtle and complex interactions between the organization and whatever surrounds it. One advantage of the open system definition is that it forces the question of what the organization is deciding/not deciding and doing/not doing to achieve its measurable results. In other words, the center stage is more likely to be filled, not with numbers, but with goals and objectives out of which flow deployment of resources for designated activities. This open system definition of growth and decline increases the chances that fundamental matters such as organizational mission would be regularly revisited.

Contrasting Schwinn and Sears

Schwinn Bicycle, as we saw above, did not adapt to major social changes in bicycle use until it was bankrupt and then purchased by another bicycle company. Under the concepts that we are using, we would conclude that Schwinn's decline began when it continued to manufacture the same kinds of bicycles and market them the same way, in spite of the evidence that the population's tastes and habits were changing. In other words, the decline did not begin simply in the quarter in which sales and profits first began to slip. It had begun months or years earlier, when the opportunity to consider shifts in the market was ignored or dismissed. Sears Roebuck was facing a similar fate. However, top decision-makers at Sears were willing to institute some significant adjustments—in this case, through selling related companies and reducing the workforce. As a result, the company repositioned itself in the department store market and began to see its profits return.

A Church That Tuned Out

Especially when the environment changes as much as it sometimes can, most established congregations find it very challenging to be flexible. The impending result is decline. Wolf Point Church, a long-established church in an urban neighborhood, watched a typical change in its immediate surroundings: the age and ethnicity of its neighbors changed. Longtime members moved farther and farther away; one even drove sixty miles to attend! On a given Sunday, a sanctuary that could seat three hundred held fifteen in the sanctuary and another fifteen in its aging choir.

During an interim pastorate, the congregation's leaders decided that they wanted to try to grow. They had already rented out part of the building to a Spanish-speaking holiness congregation; this decision came with much thought and some resistance, with finances swinging the vote. Now the ninety-year-old congregation hoped to attract more younger members, like the three in their late thirties who had joined in the last two years. All three continued after an initial visit because of how friendly a number of the members had been—all lifelong members of an ethnic clan that was intermarried. The church board decided to engage a consultant for a few months, to help them look ahead.

In the consulting process, church members talked about their own history, evaluated their traditions and values as a church, identified biblical and theological beliefs that were important to them, and gathered data on participation trends (membership, attendance, etc.) and their changing community. From the conversation between these elements, the members were asked to discern a fresh vision for their congregation. Their consultant reported later that, before this process was completed, he could sense that it was not taking hold. Before the final get-together, one of the active members told the consultant that the church was wasting its time and money. The others involved in the process were going through the motions but not identifying any new insights that would help them for their future. It was as though they expected somehow that something could just happen to increase their membership.

On the last visit, when those members who worked most actively in the process reported on their work, a lifelong member of the congregation stood up and asked the consultant, "Can we grow?" Pausing for an instant, the consultant replied, "That is up to you," summarizing again what they had worked on and how it could help them look ahead in new ways. Willingness to do so, however, was not evident. In a subsequent letter to the congregation's church board, the consultant outlined their process again and how they could use it; he offered to meet with them again, for follow-up, but received no reply.

ETHOS: ORGANIZATIONAL CULTURE AND ITS CHARACTERISTICS

Our final concept for this chapter has been popularized somewhat in recent years but still needs explanation. It is the concept that organizations themselves bear, create, and transmit culture. In chapter 3, we discussed in some detail the broad concept of culture, looking at several cultural concepts that anthropologists have developed in order to understand particular communal behavioral phenomena. Since about 1970, an increasing number of students of organizational behavior have recognized that cultural concepts also reveal significant insights about the specific experiences of organizations. Interestingly, perhaps, many of these organizational observers have taken as their subjects profit-making companies. It seems that culture tells us a lot about life as humans!

Enough was said in chapter 3 about culture that repetition here is not necessary. What we are seeking to understand at this point is the notion that, in spite of all their efforts to be rational, well-informed, organized, skilled, efficient, productive, and so on, even organizations at their core are driven by something else. That "something else" is the irrational or prerational characteristics that an organization lives out, through its stories, values, beliefs, location, space, rituals, ceremonies, heroes, and so forth. Deal and Kennedy's book, *Corporate Cultures*[14] makes the culture of organizations come alive in a way that is quite accessible to churches.

Ethos: Common Patterns

One general clarification about the use of the term will be valuable. I am applying the word "ethos" here to refer to what is known in the field more generally as organizational culture. It can be applied two ways: one, to the very idiosyncratic style or an organization, based largely upon its particular history; or, two, to more general patterns of features that organizations share in common, and that can and usually do change over time. For our purposes here, we will stay with the second application, because of my social scientific interest in seeking what I call "common patterns" of organizational behavior. That is, for instance, we can speak of common patterns that are evident in the experience of a new organization, virtually regardless of its initial purposes. Similarly, as we have seen just above, different kinds of common patterns also appear in well-established organizations. It is the insight that much group behavior is similar to other behavior arising from similar circumstances that undergirds this use of the term "ethos."

To illustrate, Deal and Kennedy's typology for organizational culture is developed from a quadrant grid created by distinguishing between two factors: how much of a chance the organization takes in doing what it does (degree of risk); and how long it takes for the organization to find out how well their activity is working (speed of feedback) (Deal and Kennedy, chapter 6). This grid creates a typology of four cultures that in actuality are mixed within most organizations. Briefly, the four are:

- Macho: high risk and quick feedback (e.g., the entertainment industry)
- Work/play hard: low risk, quick feedback (e.g., sales)
- Bet-your-company: high risk, slow feedback (e.g., mining, oil, investments)
- Process: low risk, slow feedback (e.g., banking, insurance, much government)

This particular model might not reveal as much about congregations as other models might, since risk and feedback might not be quite as salient factors for congregations as for businesses and governments. As one typology, however, it nonetheless raises our awareness about the usefulness of discovering common organizational patterns that are driven by culture.

Congregational Ethos: The Challenge for Vitality

In simple terms, a healthy organization is one that can engineer what it is doing while staying fresh and alert. It is the general purpose of this chapter to persuade you that the same basic features of any modern organization apply also to congregations. Consequently, one way that congregations can benefit from organizational insight about their existence is by striving for this same creative balance. In this section, we look at how that balance can be understood and nurtured in terms of the congregation's ethos.

As I stated earlier, we are using the term "ethos" in a more formal, rather than simply a substantive, way. That is, we seek here not to list all the possible combinations of specific, unique sets of "folkways" that region, ethnicity, denominational background, and particular history can and do create within congregations. Such a list would be overwhelming, even though we could discern some common patterns. Instead, "ethos" is used here to describe a host of features that can be measured and observed because the phenomenon in question is an organization. Deal and Kennedy, as we saw, grid these features out in terms of degree of risk and speed of feedback, but we are not limited by this quadrant.

McCann, for instance,[15] offers a cube typology, with the three factors of environment, membership, and technology. Adizes[16] proposes a quadrant based upon the two factors of the duration of activity (short-term vs. long-term) and the goal for results (efficiency vs. effectiveness). Schein[17] frames organizations in terms of culture, arguing for three levels, from the most obvious (artifacts) to the most hidden yet most important (shared basic assumptions), with a middle level (espoused values) that can be misleading. Similar, simple theoretical versions of organizational ethos can be found elsewhere. With the definition used here, we can assert similarities in ethos between congregations and secular organizations.

Seeing Ethos in Both Worlds

Such comparisons can be quite instructive. A woman at a training event that I was conducting sought me out during a break to tell me of one such connection. She was a health care administrator who had moved from a smaller company to a large, older, and more well-known one. My comments about organizational decline as a function of response to changes in the environment rang true to her new job experience. Although I had been speaking of the common problem of churches getting stuck in the mud and not wanting to change, she immediately saw the same thing occurring at the staid, respectable company that now employed her. Finding cost-effective ways of containing medical costs has been a major national issue for a number of years. Yet this woman found that the employees and managers in her new company were having a very difficult time grasping new concepts that would help them design their services in better ways. Being an experienced professional in the field who came in from outside the big company, she had no trouble understanding the issues facing it. Her new colleagues, however, we so accustomed to familiar procedures, goals, company values, and the like that the possibility of a fresh perspective escaped them.

This health professional was also a member of a church where a new angle on their ministry was needed. A core of founding members, all now retired, sincerely could not understand why they should have to do anything differently. Never mind that the church had not grown numerically for many years, even though its community had more than doubled in size! In her case, there were enough newer members in the congregation to realize that some new focus—in their case, nothing drastic—would attract new people and still be grounded in Christian identity.

This anecdote implies, correctly so, that a church's ethos will change over its lifetime. The "formal" features of ethos that make a young, up-and-coming business look and feel much like a young, up-and-coming congregation eventually lead both kinds of organizations to shift into institutionalization. For an overcontrolled organization to recreate a movementlike ethos—that is, to be adaptable—momentum must be created within a smaller group of that organization. Our health administrator friend was part of such a group in her church and recognized that "business as usual" was not going to nourish its chances for new vitality.

All approaches to ethos assume that it is not driven primarily by the reason and logic that our modern age has tried to maintain at great usefulness. Ethos, as a form of culture, is irrational, or nonrational, or perhaps prerational. In no way does this mean that ethos is inferior to rationality or efficiency. In fact, the sheer, massive persistence of culture as a human phenomenon repudiates optimistic modern assumptions such as "Science can solve all of our problems." Science itself, as a worldview and tool of modernity, also falls under the sway of culture, as Thomas Kuhn suggests in his classic essay, *The Structure of Scientific Revolutions*.[18] This same quality of culture is at least as evident in congregations as it is in any other organization, no matter how "rational" any of them strives to be.

Not Convincing Enough

Recall the story in chapter 3 about the two declining congregations who spent a year discussing what a merger would look like. The focus of their conversation was on the financial and logistical benefits of such a merger. Little, if any, was mentioned of what it would be like and feel to become one. The task force—representing both congregations—did not talk about their respective congregations as communities, as tradition-laden organizations closely tied to particular buildings and contexts. It did not share stories of their communal experiences, events, and persons who defined both congregations' earliest sense of their identities and mission. Neither did the task force share theological, spiritual, and biblical understandings of being God's people yesterday and today. All of these features of culture, of an organization's ethos, were basically ignored during the merger talks. And at least the denominational staff person who led the process realized when it was all over that it did not work; something had been missing.

What had been missing was a strategic recognition of the power of congregational ethos. Two declining congregations are incapable of making a beneficial decision about their futures, based simply upon the "facts" of finances and upkeep. This story illustrates through failure the way in which ethos can resist rationality.

Leading a Strong Ethos

Throughout this book, I have been advocating the claim that congregations must be understood in social, not only psychological, terms. Each chapter so far has made this claim in its own way. Thus, when we think about what leadership is and what it does in congregations, our basic framework here will be socially informed as well. As I have said before, using social scientific categories to explain what churches are and do certainly does not discount or eliminate the need for theological interpretation. However, if the way that we speak theologically of congregations "hangs in the air" without some acknowledgment of its reference to the real life of human communities, then it will be less helpful. It might not even be true. The same statement can be made about leadership: we want it to act out of clear awareness of who is being led, not just why.

"The Eye Cannot Say to the Hand . . ."

For one thing, leadership for vital congregational ethos realizes that neither the pastor nor the congregation can be effective without the other. Congregations whose pastors are interested in the status quo will not be able to deal creatively with the future. The reverse is also true: if the pastor is the only person in the congregation open to the future, the congregation will not move ahead. In fact, both of these scenarios are ripe for contests and conflicts! It takes a commitment to creative tension (control-adapt continuum) in the midst of contextual realities, on the part of both the pastor and the congregation, to work on an ethos that stays fresh and vital.

When pastors get together and begin to speak honestly about their work, they often share stories of their attempts to initiate change. It seems to be so much a part of the church landscape of the last generation or so that pastors feel a certain level of frustration in trying to lead. The stories deal with Sunday school curriculum, choir music, building space available for youth, financing mission versus maintaining the building, and so on. From the perspective of organizational ethos, we come to see all these stories as symbols of the congregation's self-understanding. Leaders whose actions are perceived to challenge that self-understanding become suspect and eventually might be "disarmed." We discussed power in congregations in the previous chapter. Here we are emphasizing what ethos calls for in its leaders.

Congregations cannot share all the responsibility, however, in the matter of strengthening their ethos. Sometimes a group of lay leaders in a church is ready to respond to new things, but the pastor is not. This phenomenon probably is not as frequent as willing pastors with unwilling churches, but it does occur. In these situations, the congregation is more likely to realize that it has lost an opportunity.

Who Steers?

Such a situation took place within a congregation that had been surviving for years in a radically changed area. St. John's Church had been founded in the mid-nineteenth century in a town that rapidly grew to become a regional center of political and cultural influence. Their century-old building still suggested the grandeur sought by the upper-middle-class, Gilded Age membership who financed its construction. Ministry at St. John's historically had been fairly high profile, with appealing pulpiteers and well-funded programs. Two major demographic shifts in the city during the 1900s effectively eliminated the congregation's position as a neighborhood church. Surrounded by office and government buildings, St. John's now had to appeal to residential areas some miles from their building in order to attract members.

Still, many old-timers hung on and some numbers of newer members joined St. John's for its beautiful sanctuary and music as well as the Christian fellowship evident there. These were educated, committed Christians willing to work at a faith that expressed both aesthetic and justice interests. A downtown location and a deteriorating facility, however, continued to loom as threats. Finally, some major work that was being deferred had to be done to the building. Before that would be undertaken, however, one member of the church board persuaded it to hire a consultant, who would help the congregation draw together its vision for the future.

Pastor Stan was hardworking and well-liked as St. John's minister. He had been involved in social justice ministry since the 1960s and wanted St. John's to reach out more effectively to the needs of the poor living around the building. Stan's preaching still reflected the prophetic preaching of the 1960s, calling church members to give more of themselves, because of their faith, to the downtrodden. His pastoral style was friendly yet intense; he worked long hours, often by himself, even on his day off.

During the first part of the consulting process, members of St. John's church were engaged in some reflecting and interpreting experiences about their church and area. Participation had been strong and interest was keen. When the time came for a smaller group to pull together the church's work and discern their future vision, Pastor Stan was not able to stay on task. His comments at this point returned to earlier discussions. He questioned whether the group could produce something that the church could follow. He did not follow through on his part of the assignments. When summer came, he saw reasons to delay work on the vision discernment. Attempts by the consultant to arrange another church visit through Pastor Stan were unsuccessful. Meanwhile, the building needed attention, so the church board was forced to decide on which projects and how to fund them. Pastor Stan spoke privately of being burnt out and wanting to move.

Ironically, Pastor Stan had seemed throughout most of this process to be very interested in helping St. John's Church to create a fresh ethos. The effect of his behavior, however, was to sidetrack the process, to a point at which the most active laypeople became distracted or discouraged. If this pastor had been able to work with the church leaders through this process, the congregation could have found a fresh way to focus their life. In this case, the pastor was a key reason that the church's ethos did not get renewed.

Unity, Not Unanimity

Another insight that organizational culture suggests for church leadership is that the goal is not to keep every single person in the congregation happy about every single procedure or program. In order to maintain a strong ethos, especially in a changing environment, organizations need to reassess their mission and the activities that result from that mission. When businesses hire employees, they look for persons who support their mission; to try to do it the other way around would be impossible, if not ludicrous! The mission, as the active symbol of the organization's culture, should exist prior to recruiting those who will carry out the mission.

What tends to happen in stagnant and declining congregations is that the longtime members are so familiar with the ethos and its ways that any suggestions of change tend to be perceived as a personal threat. The more that a church member identifies with the present ethos, the more difficult it is for that member to sense that congregational change would be beneficial. Longtime members closely, almost unconsciously, relate the church's values and experiences with their own. This common phenomenon creates difficulties for changing ethos, especially if persuasive reasoning or power plays are the most common forms to prevail. But ethos can be especially resistant. Change appears as a threat to the "old guard"—it feels like something into which the old guard is being talked or forced.

Learning to Become New

From the perspective of this chapter, however, such a congregation does need to become flexible—if it intends to survive beyond the life span of its current members. In other words, if the members truly regard the Christian testimony of its congregation as of primary value, then they must be willing to set their own personal preferences about church aside enough to allow a new ethos to be born—for the congregation. This becomes one of the greatest challenges for a pastor or lay leader to encounter, and handling it with skill and wisdom seems to be the exception these days. What this book seeks to do is help readers see and use a different framework for exercising such leadership.

Another one of Douglas Walrath's accounts of leading churches through change[19] illustrates how harmful it can be for church leaders to ignore the congregation's ethos. The Winchester churches were both small, of the same denomination, two miles apart, and for years had shared the same pastor. There the similarities ended, and, in fact, had ended many decades ago. The congregation with the handsome, steepled building on the hill attracted professional people living in large houses, while the other congregation's members lived down by the river, making a living by junkyards and moving vans. Their small building needed a new paint job, but no one could risk climbing ladders anymore, and it cost too much to hire someone.

Within weeks of arriving as their new pastor, George Carpenter was eager for his two charges to merge. It all made sense—dollars and cents, that is. Costs for operating both buildings could be reduced. Additionally, education programs would be strengthened and the number of meetings would be slashed. When his ten-page detailed proposal came to the board of the riverbottom church, none of the board members could think of anything to say. George had included some provisions about use of property that were sensitive and positive, but the reasonableness of the whole idea dumbfounded them. George took their silence as approval, so—with the other church board in agreement—the merger moved ahead. George felt that he had succeeded in making a significant change.

Before long, George realized that something was wrong. Even though both congregations would remain in their own buildings for two years before property decisions would be considered, attendance at the riverbottom church, however, dropped quickly by one-third. A fight was triggered when a hilltop board member suggested that worship be ended at the riverbottom church. Then people began asking questions about the merger process. Board members began to resign. Questions about George's pastoral ability surfaced both along the river and on the hilltop. After three years, George took a pastoral position elsewhere. The merged Winchester church had lost half of its Sunday morning attendance and was eking by.

George had used a rational-legal organizational decision-making style to effect a major church change. The professionals in the hilltop church could appreciate its logic better than the riverbottom church members—especially because they had more resources from which to work. What George did not realize is that the riverbottom members had the most to lose; they must have feared in part that the merged church would absorb their distinctive identity and heritage. At one level, it can be seen that differences in socioeconomic class (see chapter 2) complicated a successful merger. Yet in terms of the young pastor's own strategy, the biggest neglect was in getting to know the congregation on its own terms. Besides, it had developed a stagnant ethos and would find any possible change threatening.

A DISARMING TECHNIQUE

One metaphor that would have helped Pastor George engage both congregations constructively is what I call the "Colombo" approach. Colombo is the main character in a series of television murder movies. A detective with the Los Angeles Police Department, Colombo looks and acts like anything but a competent professional! Sporting a disheveled trench coat, driving an old clunker of a car, showing up to interrogate murder suspects at odd hours and in unexpected situations, Colombo surprises people by his unorthodox manner. He asks a lot of questions, many of which do not make sense to the listeners, and some of which irritate the suspects. He follows up clues that seem totally unrelated to the case but which turn out to undo the true murderer. No one ever knows quite how much Colombo has figured out; he never lets on, but he never acts anything but polite—in his own bumbling way. Unlike the courtroom confessions of the Perry Mason genre, Colombo never asks anyone the "Did you kill _____ because _____ ?" question.

Certainly there are elements of the Colombo character that play for their comic style. Yet at the heart of his effectiveness as a detective is a style and set of skills that church leaders would do well to imitate. His style does not challenge people or come across as wanting to be in control. Colombo never insults those with whom he must interact, regardless of their behavior or credibility. He does not criticize what is important to them; rather, he follows along with their depiction of reality in the conversation. Colombo knows how to ask further questions that prompt listeners to confirm the implications of their viewpoint, even if those implications are not as comfortable as the viewpoint itself. His questions almost always are open-ended, so that listeners may respond to them in their own words and with the story that they choose to share. Colombo does not appear to be in a hurry, as though he has to "get to the bottom of this" right away. Neither does he seem threatened by any comments that those whom he must interview make. When "the truth" is finally revealed by those who are responsible for it, Colombo does not act surprised or gloat; his manner continues to be gracious.

Colombo's style of detective work acts as a metaphor for church leadership because it fits well with the perspective on church life that organizational culture presents. It does not attempt to intimidate those whose cooperation is necessary. It enters their world on their terms, with the wisdom that the story is theirs to tell. It knows that something must be "named" in order for truth and justice to be possible.

In chapter 3, we looked at the role of the shaman as another metaphor for church leadership. The Colombo metaphor complements the shaman metaphor, by suggesting a style by which a pastor or church leader can begin to win the trust, approval—and eventually, the granted influence—of a congregation. It is something of an irony to discover in the era of democracy that power and influence often are attained by means other than a vote! This is certainly the case in many of our congregations. We discussed power in the previous chapter; our focus here is to see the organization's culture as the overarching source of how the ability to stimulate change becomes possible.

As we have just implied, the Colombo style of leadership is not intended to define all leadership at every time. Moments in a congregation's life do arise when persons in key roles need to speak from their perspectives and of their hopes. However, this chapter would argue that, all too often, pastors and church leaders move too quickly into the "opinion-stating" mode before sensing how others will interpret and thereby receive what we say. The Colombo style encourages church leaders to enter the world of the congregation's ethos first. This leadership style is also perhaps more effective and important to utilize with a stagnant or declining church ethos, rather than one that is so new that it needs leadership to clarify and elaborate it into activities and processes.

PRAYER: REKINDLING THE PRERATIONAL DIMENSION

When ancient Israel had asked Samuel for a king, so that they could "be like other nations," Yahweh told them that it would be a two-edged sword. Creating a standing army to go along with their new monarchy might have seemed glamorous to the young nation, but surely the royal need to levy taxes would not have been attractive to the masses! Such, however, are the trade-offs when seeking to keep up with the Joneses. That desire on the part of Abraham's ancient community of faith indeed threatened the one part of their existence which was intended to be at the foundation: their trust in God. Later, the prophets would rail against the people and the king for putting their trust in political alliances rather than the One who had called, sustained, rescued, supplied, nourished, protected, and established them over the generations.

Using the tools of organizational culture also can become a two-edged sword, if church leaders fail to integrate them with theological and spiritual discipline. It is my intention all throughout this book to offer a perspective on churches that can be used with, not in place of, prayer and study. To elaborate upon the many ways that church boards, study groups, and prayer groups can contribute to a new and dynamic ethos for their congregation would move us beyond our scope here. Still, the topic is so central that I want to offer a few insights and suggestions.

For Christians, churches as culture becomes one vivid way to reframe what makes us who and what we are. We can readily identify with the notion that our organization is founded upon something other than profit, rationality, convenience, pleasure, or whatever else. Our existence is rooted in a calling from God—a story, a heritage, a way of doing and being that cannot be reduced simply to other terms. The church, if nothing else, is an ethos-driven reality.

It is also true, however, that organizational culture can and does change, and that it is possible for a congregation to achieve a strong, dynamic ethos, only to allow it eventually to turn sluggish. This understanding of church experience we have tried to present in this chapter. A congregation with a truly faith-based, dynamic ethos knows how to pray, worship, support each other, and take calculated risks. Conversely, a stagnant or declining congregation has lost this skill as a community, even when there are members in its midst whose personal devotional life is vibrant. Prayers that are all form and no life-connecting substance do more harm to a congregation than good. The challenge is that prayer would become the way that church leaders connect their discernment of the future with the One whose power makes that discernment worthwhile and achievable.

This is one place where the term "prerational" or "irrational" ties into a strategy for renewing ethos. Discussions and decisions about a revitalized ethos need to be laced through with the prayers of those who lead it. In particular, the leaders need to learn how to pray together about their congregation. Their task is not to make rational decisions; it is to seek to hear and follow the leading of the Holy Spirit.

One church board got to a point that it suspended for one full year any discussion of programs, activities, finances, and votes, except for the bare minimum required by polity and law. Instead, they spent their monthly meetings in Bible study, discussions of theological and spiritual matters, and prayer. It took a few months to get used to the experiment but, when the year was finished, the results were evident. Board members had grown significantly in their biblical knowledge and understanding, in their theological comfort, in their prayer lives. New energy and ideas for ministry emerged. The congregation was on the verge of a renewal, of claiming a fresh ethos.

CONCLUSION

Congregations are organizations. In spite of their tremendous variety in tradition, location, resources, size, age, and so on, the congregations that have survived into, or emerged during, the modern world share certain organizational characteristics in common. In this respect, churches are indeed "like other nations"—and, in one respect, we can never go back. Several of these characteristics have formed the basis of this chapter: open system, environment, organization, manage-adapt continuum, decline, and ethos. Taken together, they perhaps help paint a new picture for the reader of a congregation, on a backdrop and stage that was set in chapters 2 and 3.

What makes this particular angle on "churches as organizations" somewhat new is that it does not rely upon early mechanistic models, in which efficiency, hierarchy, expertise, and so forth dictate the organization's operation. Neither does this perspective reduce a church to networks of individuals whose personal needs must be satisfied in order to make the church strong. It is certainly true that—at times in any church's life—efficiency, division of labor, training, and personal satisfaction play important roles. Yet an ethos-based model of church shifts the focus from a well-greased machine or a warm-and-fuzzy office atmosphere to a more comprehensive context: the culture that the church—as an organization—interacts with, creates, transmits, and even changes.

SEVEN

CLAY JARS

Reflections on Ministry Practice

It was the last night of class. For nine weeks, the students had been reading books that related social scientific methods and concepts to religious organizations. I had assigned them case study work on their home congregations—to collect statistical data about worship attendance and membership trends, organizational structure, and the like; to "participate-observe" the more qualitative, nuanced aspects of the congregation as they are revealed in worship, fellowship, meetings, and other activities; to gather both "hard" and "soft" data on their church's town or neighborhood; and, drawing upon insights from the social sciences, to develop an outline of what strategies would help their congregation stay healthy and vital. Now it was time to get some feedback on their impressions of the course material and its relevance for pastoral ministry.

So, first thing, I asked them to comment on what they thought of the course. Since this was the first time that it had been offered at this seminary, I wanted to know, in part, how it had made sense to them in the context of their other studies. There was a short pause in the room before Diana spoke. Diana was almost ready to graduate, a second-career seminary student, alert and capable, active in her large, dynamic African American congregation. Staring down at her notes on the desk, Diana simply declared, "I'll never look at a church the same way again!"

As a result of her study in that course, Diana had experienced a sort of epiphany. It was, I believe, the same epiphany that I had experienced some years before, the epiphany that had led me to propose to the seminary's dean that this course be offered. It was the same epiphany that has led to the writing of this book.

If you have read the entire book up to this point, perhaps you can appreciate Diana's statement. She had begun to understand the potential for church leadership that is available through the social sciences. They offer another set of lenses for perceiving our churches—or, in the metaphor from chapter 1, another set of tools for the church leader's toolbox. People who wear corrective lenses to some degree are seeing things literally in a new way. Someone who learns a trade must become proficient with certain tools, whether for woodworking or computer programming. In an analogous way, this book gives you the opportunity to learn a new trade—or, more perhaps accurately, to become more effective at a trade that you already practice, church leadership. They are tools that could lead you to say along with Diana, "I'll never look at a church the same way again!"

Each of the five preceding chapters has introduced concepts from a particular social scientific discipline and showed how those concepts can reveal certain congregational dynamics. In this final chapter, we will address the matter of application and practice more directly. It is not possible in one volume to apply concepts from several disciplines to the wide range of issues involved in congregations and then say that we are done. Churches are too complex for that, and each discipline's application could be developed more fully on its own. Hence, we seek here not to exhaust the possibilities but to illustrate and suggest them. In this regard, this chapter extends the practical focus that is introduced by the vignettes within each chapter.

Perhaps the first issue involved in using new tools is to clearly understand what they are and how they function. I will suggest in the following pages several ways that you can familiarize yourself with these concepts and their application, so that you become comfortable with them (remember the first time that you used a computer?). Then we will take up five issues that most pastors and other active church people will recognize readily as common to their church's life and task. Two of them are programmatic, that is, they constitute regular activities in the life of most churches: religious education and preaching. The other three are issues or challenges in congregations that have been receiving increasing attention over the last decade: conflict, decision-making, and renewal/vitality. Through some discussion of these five topics, the reader should begin to see even more ways that a sociocultural perspective on congregations stimulates leadership for effective churches.

GETTING TO KNOW THE TOOLS

One of the simplest ways to get conversant with the concepts in this book and the perspective that they promote is to give attention to normal church activities in a new way. How can a social scientific discipline help you to interpret usual church phenomena in a different way? How does this different way give you new insight into a specific phenomenon, why it is important, and how it can be utilized?

Consider, for instance, participation in Sunday worship. When people have told me over the years why they "go to church," the most common responses fall into three categories. They go to:

- have an oasis of peacefulness and rest amidst a hectic life;
- get inspired and lifted up;
- receive practical advice from the sermon that can be applied during the week.

These are all important functions for worship. The question is, are they the only ones? In a society that values individualism, perhaps. With a heavy emphasis upon "the self," Western societies have a tendency to place a priority on private experience. That has meant religion with a large dose of introspection.

What happens instead, however, once a religious phenomenon such as Sunday worship is viewed from the approach of sociology

or anthropology? It is not so much that personal religious experience is ignored or belittled as that it is located on a much broader
stage. Now when I go to a worship service, I am much more aware
of such realities as:

- a collection of people (social group);
- a community with a particular history;
- rituals and ceremonies, using myths and symbols;
- stories about heroes and villains.

These realities reflect more of the action, shall we say, of worship. They call attention to aspects of the experience that perhaps
are so taken for granted that their power to inform and uplift has
been lost. You can become more aware of this dimension of your
church's worship—and many of its other elements—by using concepts other than individualistic ones to help you process what you
observe.

This means that you have to be prepared at times to detach
yourself somewhat from the experience, at least enough to imagine
what things might look like for someone who just walked in the
door for the first time. Detaching, or "stepping out" a little, is a
technique that you can teach yourself. Most of us do not stay completely focused during worship or church meetings anyway! I am
encouraging you to use some of that kind of time to see some things
in another way.

We learn new insights not only by our own observation, but also
by sharing with others. You might know of someone in your congregation who would enjoy the challenge of learning new concepts
and seeing how they help you understand what goes on in your
church. You could agree to use a selected chapter or concepts with a
certain event and then meet afterward to discuss it in light of those
concepts. Asking yourself a question like, "How do we see this event
differently because of these concepts?" will concentrate your powers
of observation and recall. Checking your analysis against someone
else who was involved is a useful way to sharpen your skill.

This same learning method could be used with a group of church
leaders in a similar way. Church officers could immerse themselves
during a retreat setting with social scientific concepts, practicing their
application to real-life church situations. Conversations like this

could be very helpful in guiding the officers to make decisions about goals and plans for ministry. Pastor groups could devote a set time during their regular gatherings to discuss and apply a few concepts to their various situations. Over a period of time, officers and pastors could shift away from the tools themselves to substantive issues.

Let us take, for an example, very briefly, an issue that continues to be an actor on the public stage of American life: cultural diversity. Up until about the middle of the twentieth century, there was a sense that the national public arena was dominated by white, mostly Protestant-driven values, customs, and behaviors. Since the 1960s, even the small town in which I grew up has become more aware and tolerant of people of different color, nations, and cultures. This kind of diversity flies in the face of homogeneous, tradition-bound communities and the churches that they spawned.

How can church leaders gather resources that will be appropriate and effective with their congregations in dealing with diversity, without tearing them apart? Part of the answer, I submit, is in utilizing the social sciences. Their ability to illuminate by description offers a more neutral, often sobering, but usually very realistic picture of the way that things are. "The way that things are" will describe not only the nature of the churches themselves, as social groups with organizational culture. It also describes, more honestly than many churches seek, the nature of the environment in which the churches live—economically, socially, culturally. This is a picture that can get clouded by the passion of theological conviction that is not grounded in actual circumstances. A religious mission needs to know what it is facing, if it is to address a calling and expect to see results. Motivated groups of pastors and other church leaders can use the findings of this kind of internal and external examination to ask themselves whether their theology and practice are consistent.

Anyone who uses a workbench at home realizes that the value of tools increases when one knows how to use them together. As you get used to noticing evidence of class and status in your congregation, for example, you could also become aware of how specific features of culture vary between classes. Such variations could be operating, perhaps subtly, even within the congregation. You also might then note ties between congregational culture and the exercise of power. Decisions of several kinds can be linked together in a church by a common bond of culture, even though few persons involved would articulate the situations that way. These brief illustrations point out how interconnections between sociocultural concepts can strengthen and broaden our appreciation for our church's sometimes amazing complexity.

Let us now look at several areas of opportunity and challenge that congregations face. These short discussions will further activate your aptitude for applying social scientific perspectives to the benefit of your congregation's life and ministry.

CONFLICT: A SOCIOCULTURAL PERSPECTIVE

Most active church people do not have to be reminded that churches experience conflict! If we are realistic, we must concede that church tension is something that at times we can anticipate. What the approach taken by this book can do for you is to reframe conflict in a way that is comprehensive enough to help you deal more effectively with all its intricacy. In many situations, church conflict is less about the individuals involved and much more about diverging, sometimes implicit, values for the congregation.

There is a tendency in church conflicts to want to blame some person or two for doing something to upset the church. It seems easier to attribute a face, a name, a certain behavior for what is perceived to be wrong. Simple explanations then lead to simple solutions. However, many times the conflict symbolizes something for the church that goes beyond the immediate circumstances. In a sociocultural, open systems perspective, we must learn to ask, "What is at stake here?" and avoid being drawn into the confusing, painful surface level of the tension. We can take advantage of the broader stage to see the present scene as part of a larger act in the drama of our congregation.

When a conflict is viewed in this way, it actually can help to moderate the escalation of tension and the consequent reduction of available options. The focus of attention moves away from simply "Who is causing the trouble," a stance which takes on the tenor of a "witch hunt," that is, someone to blame. Instead, church leaders ask themselves, "What is important about our congregation's life and ministry to which we must attend because of these incidents?" Framed in this way, the congregation is less tempted to pursue particular people as "the reason" why things went wrong. This does not mean that individual church members or staff persons are passive, that they play no role in the circumstances of the conflict, or that they never contribute to its escalation. Rather, it means that their actions are most fruitfully understood in light of the congregation as an entity itself, with its multifarious social, cultural, political, and organizational dynamics.

Take the story of Bavarian Church, told in chapter 5. It would have been easy for persons on both sides of the pending vote on buying the adjacent property to frame the situation merely in terms of individuals' preferences. On such a scale, we can imagine what people in favor of the purchase might think about those who opposed it. Proponents might say that the others were old-fashioned, stubborn, or unreasonable about the opportunity, afraid to move into the future. Conversely, opponents might say of purchase supporters that they were irresponsible, that they wanted to take too big of a risk, that they would be wasting the church's hard-earned savings on something that did not have the entire congregation's support, or that certain board members just had to have their own way.

This kind of situation is not uncommon, is it? I have listened to comments like this in a number of churches over the years. Persons on both sides of a congregational issue seem to take some comfort in drawing up psychological categories of motive to explain why their church is having trouble. One danger of this stance is that, when the difference of opinion is not quickly settled, it can deteriorate into a clash of personalities and wills. The more that people get upset, the harder it is to keep the issues clearly in focus.

In seeing the congregation as an earthen vessel, church leaders instead can frame conflict on a scale that better represents the situation's complexity. A question like, "What is at stake here?" steers leaders to seek out the different sets of values that are shared to some degree, even implicitly, among the congregation. Such values grow out of members' social conditions and locations that vary. With such a scale, leaders in the Bavarian Church might come to realize that old-time members and newcomers approach the vote on property purchase differently. Longer members are mostly around retirement age and look at their town more as it used to be in years gone by. They are satisfied with what the church provides them through worship, fellowship, and other activities. Having been raised during the Great Depression, Bavarian's older members tend to be very careful with their material resources. They have been prudent savers and expect that their church will exercise similar prudence in its financial matters.

Bavarian Church's newer members tend also to be its younger ones. They were attracted to its warm, extended-family atmosphere, but they also are more inclined to focus upon future opportunities. With less history among Bavarian, the newer members are stimulated by what the church could be doing, rather than dwelling on the past. They look at their town more the way that it is now, with many first-generation families dying and their houses being purchased by young couples and singles, many of whom are moving into town for the first time. For many of Bavarian's newer members, property that is adjacent to their facility and immediately available for use is a wonderful opportunity to use church funds to expand ministry.

These contrasts between Bavarian Church's older and newer members will sound very familiar in many congregations. The point to lift up here is that, once church leaders recognize the ways in which these kinds of dynamics influence conflict, the matter of how to work through the differences moves out of the realm of personality. I would venture to speculate that most church conflict is not about individuals—although it obviously engages individuals. Rather, conflict arises when the community's own self-understanding is put to the test by action that might seem to have nothing to do with "who we are."

Using Bavarian Church's story does not imply that every sociocultural scale in congregations is measured in terms of generational differences. This does appear, however, to be one of the most common ways that this scale eventually surfaces. I encourage you to use other concepts from the chapters to imagine how to frame other conflict scenarios with which you are familiar.

DECISION-MAKING

Committees, committees, committees! Persons who become active in churches today know what it is like to participate in committees. Organizational layouts for many congregations can seem as complicated as a business corporation. How many church officers have silently wished that they could do ministry without the hassle of committees?

The committee structure that has become so familiar in churches is something of a modern phenomenon. To a large degree, it is a product of the democratization process that grew with the development of the United States. If people could vote for their officials and have recourse to government, eventually the idea for a similar kind of participation made its way into churches. With the tremendous surge of organizational development in business and industry during the first half of the twentieth century, it should come as no surprise that organizational expansion occurred almost simultaneously in many churches. This was the case especially for those denominations whose members were most likely to be involved occupationally in business and industry, for example, most mainline Protestant traditions.

There are some clear benefits for modern churches in using organizational structure that it "borrowed" from the secular world. For one thing, people will be familiar with it, since it permeates the work world. For another, it can encourage participation by more members, who can have a say in various decisions. When someone is invested in a project by helping to design it, that person is more likely to stay involved and encourage others to participate as well.

Yet, as the opening comments of this section suggest, committee experiences in congregations are not always rewarding. Sometimes the meetings are not run well; it seems in the church that we assume that adults implicitly know how to make a meeting effective. Sometimes certain church committees and boards gain reputations for being dominated by one or two persons, who don't want to listen to the ideas of others. Most pastors spend a significant amount of time (usually in the evening, when most people would rather be home) attending church meetings. The issue that we raise here is about this kind of process as effective decision making for congregational ministry.

In chapter 6, on organizational theory, we distinguished between three schools of emphasis, emerging in different generations of the twentieth century: the rational-legal school, the human relations school, and the open systems school. The ways in which decisions are made in each school of emphasis will differ, because of differences in how organization is construed. When applied to congregations, the rational-legal model organizes the church on the basis of a clear division of labor and structure, with rules and procedures, discrete positions requiring special training, a concern for being efficient and logical, written records, and the like. To get to a decision through this model, issues are worked on at a committee level; written recommendations are voted upon and pass to the church's primary governing board. Persuasion toward a decision is based upon consistency with written goals.

While the rational-legal model can be useful to a congregation, taken en toto it becomes troublesome and frustrating to employ. As a model of organizations, it does not take into account certain features of a congregation that will modify its application. One of those features, at least in the modern Western world, is that churches are voluntary associations (see chapter 2). Increasingly, persons choose whether to participate in a church and, if so, which one—and even which activities. Church choice is not like one's family identity, into which one is born. Nor is it even like a job, over which a person in the West has some selection and to which a person gives a limited kind of commitment. As a voluntary association, a congregation is not the same as many other organizations. Hence, its way of figuring out what it will do cannot be locked in strictly by an organizational model that was developed for high productivity and low cost.

The same is true for the human relations model of organizations. Aspects of this model have benefited churches—I am not arguing to the contrary. The attention to such areas as the overall conditions, motivation, productivity, and satisfaction of the organizational participant have helped church leaders develop such programs as training for officers and committee members. It has sensitized pastors and other church leaders to the importance of making committee work engaging and rewarding. One serious limitation of this model, however, is its scope. It was designed to help factory workers feel better about their jobs and so be more productive with their work time.

I would hope that church leaders have a larger vision of the purpose of church membership! Testimony to the Christian gospel is not predicated on simply finding fresh persons to fill slots in the church's program life. Yet, even without appealing to theological convictions (which are vitally important), we can find concepts in the present volume that would suggest a need to place the human relations model in a larger context. Perhaps the most telling of these concepts is that of culture. At the heart of what a congregation is, we discover a fascinating—sometimes painful—collage of history, beliefs, stories, values, special places, rituals and ceremonies, heroes, norms, and the like. In making decisions, a church's goal is not to help members feel good—although, to some extent, that is an appropriate by-product. The goal instead is to have a strong ethos, so that decisions are made on the basis of a clearly understood and valued sense of congregational identity and purpose.

This kind of goal seems to me to be at the heart of Charles Olsen's book, *Transforming Church Boards into Communities of Spiritual Leaders.*[1] In this book, Olsen uses several case churches to describe a process that creates within the board life what he calls "worshipful work." Instead of church meetings that are driven by "Robert's Rules of Order" and led (perfunctorially) by pastors who experience administration as a burden, Olsen asserts that the vitality of the congregation ought to be nurtured in its primary board. The overall tone and purpose of these meetings should be spiritual and theological. Olsen suggests several techniques for developing this style—this ethos—in the board, including personal faith sharing, congregational stories, hymn-singing, group reflection on biblical texts, and the like. His aim, however, is not for the techniques simply to be imitated, but for church boards to develop a way to discern God's leading. Discerning is not the same as voting or even as building consensus. Discernment takes time to "learn." It depends upon a robust theological culture that has been nourished within the congregation.

Olsen's book provides many rich ideas on how to make the decision-making process in a congregation be guided powerfully by its spiritual life. My purpose in referring to his book here is because it illustrates theologically the issue of decision making in a way that is parallel to the stance of this book. The pulses of our congregations are not stimulated by rational rules or motivational techniques. They depend instead upon realities of collective human experience that are revealed significantly in sociocultural terms. When these realities are integrally linked with lively theology in a biblical tradition, we have the phenomenon known as "church."

Olsen's vision for church boards calls forth much time, energy, and focus. It is a vision consistent with the theme of this book and worthy of commitment from church leaders. On the basis of the concepts described in previous chapters, I add several comments and admonitions that should help you in transforming your church's decision-making processes. First, there is nothing inherently wrong with increasing member participation through committees, discussions of proposals, task forces, votes, and so forth. In a macroculture with a strong myth of democratic freedom, it is reasonable—and can even be beneficial!—to involve church members in decision making. Second, remember that churches today are indeed voluntary associations. Persons join and take part more because they want to than that they have to. This means that commitment, enthusiasm, and engagement are generated by choice. A congregation cannot be healthy without this kind of voluntary involvement.

Third, church leaders would do well to orchestrate all processes for making decisions out of an understanding of sociocultural insights. For example, it is not wise to force votes on key issues. It is better, when circumstances allow (and they usually do, if leadership is creative and wise), to fashion a mechanism for laying out the various facets of the issue and sharing openly about them. Not everyone in the congregation with opinion-shaping influence currently sits on a voting board. And experienced pastors know that when church members get wind of something that could be controversial, they talk to each other! What you want to do is to channel that interest and conversation constructively. There is value in seeking out some of these "power brokers" early on and discussing not only the issue itself, but also ways to proceed. If Robert's Rules, or some other formal procedure, is necessary, try to use it to enhance the process, not to dictate it.

RELIGIOUS EDUCATION

In viewing religious education from the vantage point of the congregation as a clay jar, a shift of focus becomes clear. This shift is a matter of emphasis rather than of substance, strictly speaking, yet its implications for the church's educational task will be pivotal. Religious education that takes the congregation seriously not only aims at the spiritual and moral development of individuals; it also seeks to support the life of the congregation itself. This means that the way that the congregation behaves as a community of faith is just as important a subject for Christian nurture as is the guidance of private devotion and interpersonal action.

Each step in the educational process and experience will be affected by this shift of emphasis. It will guide the selection of goals for educational ministry, along with the curriculum and resources that are employed. It will shape the kinds of programs, events, and activities that the congregation understands as educational. It will counsel the ways in which leaders are trained and supported. An open system, organizational culture view of congregations will not blindly follow a "schooling" model of religious education.

The effectiveness of this approach can be illustrated by Bill Myers' ethnographic study of the youth ministry programs of two large, active Protestant congregations, one black and one white.[2] For the white congregation, known as St. Andrews, the overall function of youth ministry serves to enculturate teens into the values of dominant middle-class society. This function is not stated as a goal for St. Andrews; it is implicit but nonetheless quite evident. For the black congregation, known as Grace, the overall purpose of youth ministry is clearly stated, as a corollary to the congregation's vision. That purpose is to help young people critique the culture around them, developing a sense of Christian identity deeply informed by their black heritage. Whereas youth in the active ministry at St. Andrews experience (macro) cultural reinforcement, youth at Grace experience (macro) cultural suspicion and development/celebration of a (meso) cultural alternative.

Myers' analysis continues by summarizing and contrasting the "teaching agendas" of the two congregations. Whereas St. Andrews implicitly teaches adherence to macrocultural values, Grace explicitly teaches distinctive values blending Christian theology and African American tradition. The two can be compared thusly, in five ways:[3]

ST. ANDREWS	GRACE
Being middle-class	Being unashamedly ethnic
Being morally good	Being unapologetically Christian
Being a competent manager	Being a competent adult
Being friendly	Being politically aware
Not being different	Making a life

Myers concludes that, by having developed this tacit accommodating approach to youth, St. Andrews has weakened its ability to do ministry.[4]

My point in summarizing Myers' study is not to condemn one congregation while glorifying the other one. It is rather to see in these case studies working evidence that it is important for church leaders to understand their congregations in the full context of their environments. By "understanding" here I mean insights emerging out of descriptions afforded through social scientific concepts. It could be argued that St. Andrews Church is hampered to the extent that it is not able to speak language that would allow it to see itself—and its calling for ministry—in new, more comprehensive ways. Grace Church, by contrast, has faced its sociocultural location and fosters no illusions about it. Rather, Grace has turned its macrocultural position into a key point upon which to build Christian ministry. Its willingness to accept the nature of the macrophenomenon as it is becomes a starting point, one springboard for linking up with theology to create a powerful congregational vision.

The St. Andrews/Grace comparative study suggests some different emphases and directions for congregational education. For one thing, it will be centered in developing faith-in-community, not some other, borrowed category such as age alone. Age separation in churches reinforces the schooling model of education, so heavily utilized in white church traditions. Community-centered education is more likely to support the congregation's particular ethos, as it understands itself and its calling to ministry. This kind of religious education, as is evident in Grace Church,[5] promotes ritual, symbol, and ceremony as lively resources for learning. It uses the rhythm of a defined theology within a particular heritage as keys for programming and activity. Education is less a separated-off, minimally attended option for church members and more a deliberate and central aspect of the congregation's life.

PREACHING

Preaching ministry of a congregation whose leaders perceive their church on the scale promoted here will bear a look and feel that will not necessarily seem that different, yet will be so, in a transformative way. Seeing the congregation with sociocultural eyes opens up, in dramatic ways, the dimensions of community, culture, and power within biblical texts that often go unnoticed. Sermons framed on this level relate these broader descriptive concepts about human existence to the application of textual meaning. The purpose of this method is not to impose, not to lay over the phenomenon a template that does not fit. Rather, what we begin to discover as we try out the social scientific concepts in our toolbox is that they clearly help explain important features and ideas in the texts themselves.

Over the last two decades or more, the discipline of biblical scholarship has witnessed a rise of interest in applying social scientific tools to the Bible. That literature continues to grow, and much of it concentrates on scholarly development. Some writers,[6] though, have sought to show how this sociocultural perspective on the Bible itself can help illuminate exegetical work that leads to exciting and challenging church application.

Such an appreciation of this scale of interpretation is illustrated in John Buchanan's pastoral discussion[7] of the story in John 4 of Jesus talking with the woman at the well. Perhaps the most common approaches in treating this text frame the hermeneutic in terms of individual morality and the lost soul. Here, so this line of thought goes, is a person who has made some bad choices in her life, but Jesus has caught her at her own game. Once she realizes her condition, she is ready for the salvation that is available through Christ. On this scale, the interpretation seems evident and has been applied thousands of times by churches trying to help individuals straighten out their lives.

On another scale, however—a broader scale that takes into account more of the story's own context, another distinct theme emerges. Buchanan points out, using cultural and historical categories, that Jesus meeting the woman at the well is a story set in themes that are very familiar even today: "[it] is first of all about racism and religious prejudice, a germane topic in light of escalating racial and religious intolerance and violence in our country and throughout the world."[8] This conclusion is based upon considering the location of the story, Samaria, and the historical relations between Jews and Samaritans. Jews considered themselves far superior to Samaritans, whose past included a monarchical defeat and cultural absorption by the conquering settlers. Jews had nothing good to say about Samaria; it was, in Buchanan's terms, "a despicable place." Thus, when interpreting the woman who speaks with

Jesus at the well, she not only has "fallen from grace," she is "a marginal person in an already marginalized culture."

When the preacher's understanding of biblical texts takes in this kind of sociocultural scale, the proclamatory aspect of preaching will operate at this scale as well. That is, whatever angle on the gospel that is revealed in the text is interpreted for today's listeners in the context of culture and community. Buchanan makes such a connection:

> The story of Jesus and the woman at the well is about God's welcome, God's hospitality. It is a set of marching orders for the church as it reaches out to men and women who are marginalized in our culture, racially, religiously or morally.[9]

Notice that the application does not deny relevance to persons; rather, it is the way that this relevance is grounded in a recognized context of society, culture, and history that makes it that much more germane. Such grounding is made possible by facility with tools that reveal that scale of the human phenomenon.

Preaching with this kind of awareness does not play into a common American religious dichotomy between salvation and social action. If anything, seeing our congregations as earthen vessels in this way makes the nature of proclamation seemingly more intricate. I say "seemingly" because, any time that we shift paradigms, it feels more difficult at first. Yet we can argue that social scientific tools help the preaching task take a "both-and" stance on the focus of the message. Both personal commitment and congregational witness derive their validity and necessity from the Scriptures. What most American congregations need to "see" is the relation of the personal to the collective. This is no small task for preaching, yet the future of Christian witness is at stake.

CONGREGATIONAL VITALITY AND RENEWAL

Our last topic in this chapter on ideas for practice is one that is receiving increased attention in church circles. Why do some congregations thrive and others struggle to survive? Why is it that two congregations can follow the same strategies for church growth and one will increase membership while the other will not? What are the signs of a genuinely healthy congregation? How can a church know if and when it needs to pay attention to its health?

It is one of my premises that healthy churches don't just happen. They are nourished by leaders with deep faith and a commitment to make a difference. They develop and can even change character over time. Merely because a congregation exists over time does not mean that it automatically is theologically adept and practically relevant. Congregations have been known to turn into not much more than social clubs with chapel services.

What makes a congregation healthy, faithful, and effective as a gospel witness must be defined ultimately in theological terms. That wondrous, gracious response to God's way in the world constantly reaches beyond the limits of our experience. That is part of its mystery but also of the hope that it offers. God can do in and through us more than we can ask or think. Yet such a conviction of faith too often has tried to function as though the specific world around it was of no account. Before modernity, that world was defined in purely mythological terms and often was driven by fear of powers and principalities. This was a world where definitions were simple and solutions seemed clear. In today's intellectual and cultural climate, it is still tempting, in some traditions at least, for church groups to behave as though simplistic analysis can still provide adequate worldviews from which to proclaim Christian faith.

There is no shortage today of articulate, compelling voices in theology, responding to various perspectives that have been too long suppressed. However, for church leaders looking for ministry practice, new theological norms alone usually will not be sufficient. When those norms help a congregation see themselves and their context in new ways, then genuine response and transformation is possible. This means that the congregation somehow has been able to look at itself soberly, in a manner akin to the approach of a social scientist.

I am arguing, then, that social scientific concepts can be used as mirrors for the lives and locations of our congregations. As mirrors, they reflect what they see. It is up to the viewer to evaluate what the mirror reveals. Categories of social grouping, status, power, culture, and the like help church leaders see more clearly. The concepts themselves do not dictate or even suggest what should be done about what one sees. But the image is available for those congregations who are willing to look.

In other words, social science can be used by congregations as a reality check, as a way of more honestly describing themselves and their places in the world. Such a reality check is necessary for a congregation that wants to stay healthy. Size, in itself, is not a measure of church health. Willingness and ability to bring its understanding of the gospel to bear upon life in its own environment is the acid test. Any congregation—new, young, established, or declining—can seek health using this acid test.

Let us consider with a little detail what this looks like. We have been contrasting here the descriptive role that the social sciences can take. Congregational leaders can learn to be aware of information and occurrences that could influence the church. These descriptive data will generate both from within the congregation and within its surroundings. They will be both "hard" and "soft" data—they reveal phenomena that can be measured easily with statistics, as well as aspects of the phenomena that are more elusive (survey trends, ethnic cultural patterns, etc.). All of the kinds of data help leaders assess whether circumstances, needs, and opportunities are changing. A congregation that is vital already has its ear to the ground on such matters; congregations needing renewal are in danger of losing their hearing altogether.

Regardless of a congregation's current state of health, a changing community calls for the ability to appraise what is happening (descriptive) in light of the congregation's sense of purpose (normative). The more a congregation is different from its context, the more renewal that will be required. One main reason for this axiom is that congregations usually are founded in settings where their original vision had a good chance of succeeding. A changing context is often (but not always) less conducive to that early congregational mission. Congregations that are more committed to doing what they are doing now rather than adapting to new mission opportunities are less likely to take two necessary steps. One is to look at their context and themselves with eyes wide open. Another is to entertain important options in light of honest self-assessment.

In sociological terms, the contrast between adaptive and rigid stances can be explained in part by the concepts of movement and institution (see chapter 2). If we understand these two concepts as poles of a spectrum, they become one useful tool for renewal. The challenge for any congregation is to develop itself to a place where it can exercise key features of both poles, in a productive tension.

On the other extreme, churches can be so flexible that they fall apart, as we saw with the Newton Church (chapter 6). There the pastor encouraged no institutionalizing process that would have provided some necessary congregational stability. The pastor's influence is considerable in the movementlike early years of a congregation. Another church's founding pastor retired after many years of faithful, effective service to a growing congregation. But he continued to live in town and maintain an almost daily contact with the few remaining charter members. The congregation as a whole was ready, willing, and able to adapt their vision, mission, and activities appropriately to changes occurring around them. Its new pastor had been selected for that purpose. However, influences of the founding pastor upon key old-time leaders stymied efforts for reasonable change. After several years, the congregation's talented, warm, earnest new pastor accepted another call. Several formerly active newer members (i.e., under twenty years in length) already had resigned from boards in frustration and were attending worship infrequently. In this case, the old guard was institutionalized so strongly that they were impeding congregational movement toward a new stage of healthy, dynamic Christian witness.

This congregation's unfortunate experience also suggests, as I already have intimated, what role a sociocultural awareness plays in a congregation. The tools themselves are not the gospel. There is nothing inherent in descriptive concepts of any kind that will force a lethargic or unwilling group to change its perspective. For congregations, that role must be played by theology. Even theology, however, can become rigid, as evidence in both the Bible and history bear witness! Yet the tools are very valuable, especially for the kind of increasingly complex world in which virtually all of us live. How is American macroculture different now than it was after World War II? How do those differences affect what churches might or might not be able to do, or even to assume? These questions need the less partial and more sobering descriptions that concepts from social science can furnish to church leaders.

CONCLUSION

This chapter has sought to suggest practical directions for congregational action, based upon the conceptual tools of this book. Space limits the number of topics and the extent to which they can be discussed here. Yet I hope that, by illustrating the movement from theory to practice, your own creativity to apply them will be stimulated. You are on the cusp of an exciting, sometimes difficult, but surely a rewarding adventure! We are entering a new era, for our world, our churches, and our needs for leadership.

Paul the apostle wrote to one of the first mission congregations, "But we have this treasure in clay jars, to show that the transcendent power belongs to God and not to us" (2 Cor. 4:7). That is indeed one quality that we share with our spiritual ancestors: being clay jars. Like clay pots rather than shiny metal wares, most congregations realize that they are not fancy, impressive, or inspiring in their perfection. Like clay pots, congregations are made to be useful to their maker, and can even be somewhat attractive—they are human and made of the same stuff of all humanity. Yet Paul's declaration assures that it is into such vessels that God enters. Paul wants Christians to realize that it is because of being made of mere clay that our Christian witness through churches will point to God.

APPENDIX

A Study Guide

The following questions and activities are designed for those who wish to take the ideas from this book and begin applying them in congregational ministry. Whether or not you are one kind of ministry practitioner or another, you are encouraged especially to think about how you would answer the following questions based on chapter 1. These questions function as an informal "pretest" of your perceptions and attitudes about congregational analysis and paradigms. The rest of the questions for each chapter are keyed to the concepts and ideas discussed respectively.

You might study these questions on your own, use them in a class, small group exercise, or church staff meeting or retreat; design an adult study around them; or discuss them with other colleagues in your or another denomination.

CHAPTER 1

Horseless Carriages: Why Another "New" Paradigm?

1. If you first learned how to use a keyboard on a typewriting machine, how did you feel when you first sat in front of a computer keyboard? What kind of paradigm shift were you experiencing?

2. What do horseless carriages and toolboxes have in common?

3. What paradigms have you encountered in your lifetime? How have you responded to them? How have they affected the way that you look at the world, how you live?

4. When you think about local congregations, which of the following terms help you best understand them?

Family	Social club
System	All-service
Cold and stuffy	Corporation
Chapel	Complex organization

5. How are churches in small towns and big cities like each other? How are they different?

CHAPTER 2

Beyond the Cocoon Syndrome: Congregation as Social Group

1. Using some of the concepts in this chapter, note ways in which your congregation and its neighborhood are similar to, and different from, Fieldtown and Lord Jesus Church.

Concept	Fieldtown	Your Town	Lord Jesus Church	Your Church
Social group				
Voluntary association				
Class				
Marginality				

2. With which sociological features of your congregation and community are your congregation most comfortable? About which ones does it find most difficult to talk? Why?

3. Is your church more of a movement or an institution? What evidence do you see for your assessment? What would it take to develop a creative balance between the two?

4. How can you identify ways in which your congregation is marginal? How could this marginality be used to focus your church's self-understanding and ministry?

5. What kind of fresh congregational vision of identity (who we are) and purpose (what we are to do) might a sociological understanding of your church suggest? Which are the appropriate groups and persons in your church to be engaged in such a discernment?

CHAPTER 3
Making Your Way Around the Village: Congregation as Bearer of Meaning

1. This chapter introduces quite a few concepts from cultural anthropology. Use the following selected list to think about your congregation. What fresh perspectives are suggested?

Concept	Your Church	New Insight
Microculture		
Values and norms		
Symbols		
Heroes		

2. What is the mesoculture that defines your region and/or its ethnic dominance? Is it hard to identify its features? If so, ask yourself how your part of the country is different from another part. You might feel that this is "stereotyping," but

the focus is on patterns that are widespread, rather than the specific behavior of every single person.

3. What is the cultural value in your congregation of certain space, such as the sanctuary? Fellowship area? Kitchen? Education rooms? In what ways would it be apparent that the "proper use" of these spaces had been violated? Does every group in the church agree about what is "proper?"

4. Which subculture in your church influences your congregation more than any other? What are its beliefs, values, and norms? How does it behave? Identify one other subculture in your church. What does it take for these two subcultures to work together?

5. Applying the concepts of story, ceremony, and liminality, what would you recommend to a new pastor or church member who wants to acquire a shaman role in your congregation?

CHAPTER 4
Not a Necessary Evil: Congregation as Locus of Exchange

1. What does your church understand its market to be? Primarily current members? Families of members? New residents in your town or neighborhood? Others? What does this perception of its market suggest about your congregation's operating vision?

2. What discussion would ensue among your church board over the list of market questions in the section "The Church in the Marketplace?"

3. Use the following concepts to summarize and assess your congregation's current resources and use of those resources.

Concept	Used in Congregation	Ways to Develop
Market		
Capital		
Human capital		

What might an increased understanding of economic factors that influence a congregation do to help your church board plan for the congregation's future?

4. Make a list of five active church members whom you know. Ask each one what he or she has invested in the congregation and what return each receives from it. Do the same with five inactive members whom you know.

5. How does your congregation encourage developing human capital in the areas discussed at the end of the chapter—worship, education, and fellowship?

CHAPTER 5
"But Jesus Never Talked About That!": Congregation as Collective Capacity

1. Use the several concepts from this chapter to look at your congregation. What do you see differently about it than before you considered these concepts?

Concept	Your Congregation	New Insight
POWER		
Class (economic)		
Status (social)		
Party (political)		
AUTHORITY		
Charismatic		
Traditional		
Bureaucratic		
VOLUNTARY ASSOCIATION		
GOVERNANCE (polity)		
Episcopal		
Presbyterian		
Congregational		

2. With explanation, how easily would members of your congregation recognize the presence of these "power phenomena" in your church? Which ones might they readily accept? Which ones might be more difficult for them to understand or deal with?

3. Which form of governance (polity) does your church have? How has that form influenced the way that things happen in your congregation? What informal criteria operate for filling committees and offices? How does the interaction between these formal and informal processes reflect what your church holds to be important?

4. Discuss the questions highlighted in chapter 2, in the section on class and status, with another leader in your congregation. How do your responses to these questions point to your church's strengths? To ways that it might grow, change, or improve?

5. In what ways could your church's boards and committees use this chapter on power to guide the ways that they consider, decide, and implement things? What theological ramifications can you see here for your church?

CHAPTER 6
Being "Like Other Nations":Congregation as Complex Organization

1. Use the notes that you took in the exercise at the beginning of this chapter to help you think about your church in terms of the following concepts:

Concept	Your Congregation	Insight
Environment		
Organization		
Isomorphism		
Ethos		

2. Outline a "flowchart" of how your church is organized and how things get done. This outline might include such categories as committees, boards, fellowship groups, task forces, and the like. How much of this flowchart reveals what goes on inside the congregation? What aspects of the chart point to an awareness of the congregation's environment?

3. On a straight line illustrating the range between managing and adapting, where do you think your church falls?

————————————————— X —————————————————

Tightly managed **Well-balanced** **Highly adaptable**

What would it take to move your congregation toward the middle?

4. Following the open systems definition in this chapter, do you think that your church is growing or declining? What evidence would you cite to support your assessment?

5. What "common patterns" can you identify in your congregation that express its current ethos? If you can see ways that this ethos is weak, how might you employ the "Colombo approach" to stimulate interest in keeping the church strong?

CHAPTER 7
Clay Vessels: Reflections on Ministry Practice

1. Imagine that you are a member of the governing board of a parish or local congregation. During one of the stated board meetings, another board member reports on an episode in the church that clearly indicates disagreement between two factions in the church. One group opposes the other group's request that the church's teenagers be allowed to use a certain part of the church property for a special event.

- How would a board conversation about such a report typically transpire?

- How might concepts introduced in this book help you help the board reframe the situation?

- How could this reframing lead to a more productive solution to the disagreement?
- What could the board learn through this process?

2. What features of your church's governing board would fall under which organizational model?

Rational-legal	Human relations

How do each of these features help your church in its ministry? In what ways might they hinder ministry?

3. What religious educational opportunities does your parish provide? What curricula and other resources are used? Who participates? To what extent do these offerings help your church understand its environment as context for ministry?

4. To what kind of audience does your church's preacher direct the theological aspects of his/her preaching? Primarily to individuals? How do issues of church as community, of neighborhood, town, region, nation, or world get treated in your preacher's sermons? What are some hermeneutical implications of this book?

5. Think of a church that you know well. How is it different today than it was twenty-five years ago? Which of the changes are "obvious?" Which ones are harder to see but still important? Which concepts in the book might help this church learn to stay both self-controlled and flexible? Which concepts help you understand how to deal with natural resistance to change?

ENDNOTES

PREFACE

1. Loren Mead, *The Once and Future Church: Reinventing the Congregation for a New Mission Frontier* (n.p.: The Alban Institute, 1991).

2. George B. Thompson Jr., *Futuring Your Church: Finding Your Vision and Making It Work* (Cleveland: United Church Press, 1999).

3. George B. Thompson Jr., *How to Get Along with Your Church: Creating Cultural Capital for Doing Ministry* (Cleveland: Pilgrim Press, 2001).

CHAPTER 1

1. Thomas Kuhn, *The Structure of Scientific Revolutions*, 2d ed., enlarged (Chicago: University of Chicago Press, 1970), 60.

2. Ibid., 59.

3. Ibid., 57; cf. 52–53.

4. Ibid., 55.

5. Ibid., 65.

6. Ibid.

7. Ibid., 67–68; see also 74–75.

8. Ibid., 5.

9. Ibid., ch. 8, esp. 89–91.

10. See, for instance, Loren Mead, *The Once and Future Church: Reinventing the Congregation for a New Mission Frontier* (n.p.: The Alban Institute, 1991) and *Transforming Congregations for the Future* (n.p.: The Alban Institute, 1994).

11. See, for instance, Speed Leas, *Discovering Your Conflict Management Style,* rev. ed. (n.p.: The Alban Institute, 1997), and George Parsons and Speed Leas, *Understanding Your Congregation as a System* (n.p.: The Alban Institute, 1993).

12. One of Oswald's more recent publications is with Robert E. Friedrich, Jr., *Discerning Your Congregation's Future: A Strategic and Spiritual Approach* (n.p.: The Alban Institute, 1996). His earlier short piece, *Power Analysis of a Congregation,* (n.p.: The Alban Institute, 1981), helped to open up a sociocultural perspective for me.

13. Gilbert Rendle, *Leading Change in the Congregation: Spiritual and Organizational Tools for Leaders,* (n.p.: The Alban Institute, 1998).

14. Edwin Friedman, *Generation to Generation: Family Process in Church and Synagogue* (New York: Guilford Press, 1985). Loren Mead, founder and retired president of The Alban Institute, has referred to this book as "a prime resource for judicatory executives and bishops." See Loren Mead, *Transforming Congregations for the Future* (n.p.: The Alban Institute, 1994), 135.

15. See, for instance, Peter Steinke's work, e.g., *Healthy Congregations: A Systems Approach* (n.p.: The Alban Institute, 1996).

16. For a summary of this history, especially in Chicago, see Clinton E. Stockwell, "Graham Taylor, Urban Pioneer," *The Chicago Theological Seminary Register,* 86/1 (winter 1996), 1–23.

17. See Samuel C. Kincheloe, *The Church in the City: Samuel C. Kincheloe and the Sociology of the City Church* (Chicago: Exploration Press, 1989).

18. H. Paul Douglass, *1000 City Churches: Phases of Adaptation to Urban Environment* (New York: George H. Doran, 1926), frontpiece.

19. Based upon the 1920 U.S. Census, the Institute's research team decided to study churches in cities with populations of 100,000 or more; see Douglass, *1000 City Churches,* v.

20. See ibid., xxiii.

21. Ibid., 313ff.

22. For one of the earlier summaries of research on the post-1960s era, see Wade Clark Roof and William McKinney, *American Mainline Religion: Its Changing Shape and Future* (New Brunswick, N.J.: Rutgers University Press, 1987).

23. The Chicago Area Group for the Study of Religious Communities (CAGSRC) was organized in the fall of 1991 by Carl Dudley and R. Stephen Warner. Its purpose is to foster among professors, graduate students, and practitioners social scientific research on religious organizations and movements. Warner's award-winning early study of Mendocino Presbyterian Church in California exemplifies the fruit of synthesizing ethnographic research, good writing and engaging narrative; see R. Stephen Warner, *New Wine in Old Wineskins: Evangelicals and Liberals in a Small Town Church* (Berkeley: University of California Press, 1988). For a more recent, comparative study of twenty-three congregations in nine communities undergoing demographic change, see Nancy Tatom Ammerman, et.al., *Congregation and Community* (New Brunswick, N.J.: Rutgers University Press, 1997).

24. James M. Gustafson, *Treasure in Earthen Vessels: The Church as a Human Community* (New York: Harper & Brothers, 1961), 9.

25. George B. Thompson Jr., *Futuring Your Church: Finding Your Vision and Making It Work* (Cleveland: United Church Press, 1999); and George B. Thompson Jr., *How to Get Along with Your Church: Creating Cultural Capital for Doing Ministry* (Cleveland: Pilgrim Press, 2001).

26. So many titles are available that address change and its impact on the Church that it would be fruitless here to try to name even a representative list of them. One of the more creative books in this category is Leonard Sweet's heavily footnoted *Soul Tsunami: Sink or Swim in New Millennium Culture* (Grand Rapids: Zondervan, 1999).

27. Lucien Price, *The Dialogues of Alfred North Whitehead* (New York: Mentor Books, 1954), 205.

CHAPTER 2

1. A summary of Durkheim's study can be found in Joseph McCann, *Church and Organization: A Sociological and Theological Enquiry* (London and Toronto: Associated University Presses, 1993), 21.

2. Max Weber, *The Protestant Ethic and the Spirit of Capitalism*, trans. Talcott Parsons (New York: Charles Scribner's Sons, 1958).

3. H. Richard Niebuhr, *The Social Sources of Denominationalism* (New York: Henry Holt, 1929).

4. James M. Gustafson, *Treasure in Earthen Vessels: The Church as a Human Community* (New York: Harper and Brothers, 1961).

5. McCann, *Church and Organization*, 19.

6. James Luther Adams, *Voluntary Associations: Socio-Cultural Analyses and Theological Interpretations* (Chicago: Exploration Press, 1986), 250.

7. Ibid.

8. Wade Clark Roof and William McKinney, *America Mainline Religion: Its Changing Shape and Future* (New Brunswick, N.J.: Rutgers University Press, 1987), 102.

9. See, for instance, R. Stephen Warner, *New Wine in Old Wineskins: Evangelicals and Liberals in a Small-Town Church* (Berkeley: University of California Press, 1988), 45–47.

10. W. G. Runciman, ed., *Weber: Selections in Translation,* trans. Erik Matthews (Cambridge, England: Cambridge University Press, 1978).

11. Niebuhr, *The Social Sources of Denominationalism.*

12. Runciman, *Weber*, 43–44.

13. Perry London, "The Rescuers: Motivational Hypotheses about Christians who Saved Jews from the Nazis," in J. Macaulay and L. Berkowitz, *Altruism and Helping Behavior: Social Psychological Studies of Some Antecedents and Consequences* (New York: Academic Press, 1970).

14. See C. Kirk Hadaway and David A. Roozen, *Rerouting the Protestant Mainstream: Sources of Growth and Opportunities for Change* (Nashville: Abingdon Press, 1995), chap. 2.

15. Ibid., chap. 1.

16. Ibid., 120–23.

17. William M. Easum, *Sacred Cows Make Gourmet Burgers: Ministry Anytime, Anywhere, By Anybody* (Nashville: Abingdon Press, 1995), chaps. 5ff.

CHAPTER 3

1. James Hopewell, *Congregation: Stories and Structures,* ed. Barbara G. Wheeler (Philadelphia: Fortress Press, 1987).

2. See especially Denham Grierson's anthropological teaching model for students in field education, *Transforming a People of God* (Melbourne: Joint Board of Christian Education, 1984); see also Nancy Ramsay's briefer exploration of the same theme in "The Congregation as a Culture: Implications for Ministry," *Encounter*, 53/1 (1992), 36–46.

3. See Robert Worley's early efforts in *A Gathering of Strangers: Understanding the Life of Your Church* (Philadelphia: Westminster Press, 1976).

4. See Serena Nanda, *Cultural Anthropology,* 2d ed. (Belmont, Calif.: Wadsworth Publishing, 1984), 5.

5. Ibid., 67.

6. Andrew M. Pettigrew, "On Studying Organizational Cultures." *Administrative Science Quarterly* 24/4 (1979), 574.

7. These researchers, with references, include Charles Perrow, *Complex Organizations: A Critical Essay,* 3d ed. (New York: McGraw-Hill. 1986), see chap. 1; Paul J. DiMaggio and Walter W. Powell, "The Iron Cage Revisited: Institutional Isomorphism and Collective Rationality in Organizational Fields," *American Sociological Review* 48 (1983), 147–60; Harrison M. Trice, "Rites and Ceremonials in Organizational Cultures," in *Research in the Sociology of Organizations: A Research Annual,* vol. 4 (Greenwich, Conn.: JAI Press, 1985), 221–69; and John W. Meyer and Brian Rowan, "Institutionalized Organizations: Formal Structure as Myth and Ceremony," *American Journal of Sociology* 83/2 (1977), 340–63.

8. Nanda, *Cultural Anthropology,* 67.

9. Ibid., 297–98.

10. Ibid., 303.

11. Terrence E. Deal and Allen A. Kennedy, *Corporate Cultures: The Rites and Rituals of Corporate Life* (Reading, Mass.: Addison-Wesley, 1982), 39–40.

12. Nanda, *Cultural Anthropology,* 300–01.

13. Douglas Walrath, *Leading Churches Through Change* (Nashville: Abingdon Press, 1979), 36–40.

14. For a very thorough, fascinating discussion of generational theory and American history, see William Strauss and Neil Howe, *Generations: The History of America's Future, 1584–2069* (New York: Quill/William Morrow, 1991).

15. As quoted in Denham Grierson, *Transforming a People of God,* 3.

16. Nanda, *Cultural Anthropology,* 315.

CHAPTER 4

1. A sympathetic and practical presentation of marketing practices, written by business teachers with congregational and pastoral experience, is offered in Norman Shawchuck, et al., *Marketing for Congregations: Choosing to Serve People More Effectively* (Nashville: Abingdon Press, 1992).

2. R. Stephen Warner, "Work in Progress toward a New Paradigm for the Sociological Study of Religion in the United States," *American Journal of Sociology,* 98/5 (March 1993), 1051.

3. Nathan Rosenberg and L.E. Birdzell, *How the West Grew Rich* (New York: Basic Books, 1986), 6–9.

4. See James Luther Adams, *Voluntary Associations: Socio-Cultural Analyses and Theological Interpretations* (Chicago: Exploration Press, 1986), 250.

5. Ibid., 176–77.

6. Ibid., 177–78.

7. Rosenberg and Birdzell, *How the West Grew Rich,* 38ff.

8. Warner, "Work in Progress," 1050–51.

9. Timothy L. Smith, *Revivalism and Social Reform: American Protestantism on the Eve of the Civil War* (New York: Harper & Row, 1965), chaps. I and III.

10. Warner, "Work in Progress," 1051.

11. C. Kirk Hadaway and David A. Roozen, *Rerouting the Protestant Mainstream: Sources of Growth and Opportunities for Change* (Nashville: Abingdon Press, 1995), 40–43.

12. Ibid., 46.

13. Ibid.

14. Ibid., 47.

15. Ibid., 52; see also Penny Long Marler and David A. Roozen, "From Church Tradition to Consumer Choice: The Gallup Surveys of the Unchurched American," in David A. Roozen and C. Kirk Hadaway, eds., *Church and Denominational Growth* (Nashville: Abingdon Press, 1993), 266.

16. Ibid., 269–77.

17. Ibid., 266.

18. Ibid., 265.

19. Norman Shawchuck, Philip Kotler, Bruce Wrenn, and Gustave Rath, *Marketing for Congregations: Choosing to Serve People More Effectively* (Nashville: Abingdon Press, 1992), 379.

20. Tom Riddell, Jean Shackelford, and Steve Stamos, *Economics: A Tool for Understanding Society,* 4th ed. (Reading, Mass.: Addison-Wesley, 1991), 7.

21. Thomas H. Greer, *A Brief History of the Western World,* 5th ed. (San Diego: Harcourt Brace Jovanovich, 1987), 206.

CHAPTER 5

1. So much literature on church conflict has been generated that it would be difficult to include much of it here. Hugh Halverstadt's book,

Managing Church Conflict (Louisville: Westminster John Knox, 1991), includes a bibliography with many of the secular and religious publications to date.

2. W. G. Runciman, ed., *Weber: Selections in Translation,* trans. Erik Matthews (Cambridge, England: Cambridge University Press, 1978), 43.

3. Ibid, 43–56.

4. For a sympathetic and practical treatment of the presence of "traditional orality" in the United States, see Tex Sample, *Ministry in an Oral Culture: Living with Will Rogers, Uncle Remus, and Minnie Pearl* (Louisville: Westminster John Knox Press, 1994).

5. As indicated in Joseph McCann, *Church and Organization: A Sociological and Theological Enquiry* (London and Toronto: Associated University Presses, 1993), 57–58.

6. James Luther Adams, *Voluntary Associations: Socio-Cultural Analyses and Theological Interpretations* (Chicago: Exploration Press, 1986), 172–79.

7. James M. Gustafson, *Treasure in Earthen Vessels: The Church as a Human Community* (New York: Harper & Brothers, 1961) 38–41.

8. Clarence N. Stone, *Regime Politics: Governing Atlanta, 1946–1988* (Lawrence: University Press of Kansas), 6.

9. Ibid., 7.

10. Ibid., 7–8.

11. Ibid., 9.

12. Eric Law, *The Wolf Shall Dwell with the Lamb: A Spirituality for Leadership in a Multicultural Community* (St. Louis: Chalice Press, 1993).

13. Ibid., 18–25.

14. Ibid., 25.

15. Ibid., 73–77.

16. Ibid., 73.

CHAPTER 6

1. Lynne G. Zucker, "Organizations as Institutions," in Samuel B. Bacharach, ed., *Research in the Sociology of Organizations: A Research Annual,* volume 2 (Greenwich, Conn.: JAI Press, 1983), 14–16.

2. Max Weber, *Basic Concepts in Sociology,* translated and with an introduction by H. P. Secher (New York: Citadel Press, 1962), 108.

3. Joseph F. McCann, *Church and Organization: A Sociological and Theological Enquiry* (Scranton, Pa.: University of Scranton Press, 1993), 56–57.

4. For the summary that appears in this section, see ibid., 35–41.

5. Samuel L. Kincheloe, *The Church in the City: Samuel L. Kincheloe and the Sociology of the City Church* (Chicago: Exploration Press, 1989). 3–10.

6. Ibid., chapter 3.

7. Ibid., pp. 96–98.

8. For a consistent use of the tandem concepts of manageability and adaptability in management theory, see Ichak Adizes, *Corporate Lifecycles: How and Why Corporations Grow and Die and What to Do About It* (Englewood Cliffs, N.J.: Prentice Hall, 1988).

9. John W. Meyer and Brian Rowan, "Institutionalized Organizations: Formal Structure as Myth and Ceremony," *American Journal of Sociology* 83/2 (1977), 340–63.

10. Paul J. DiMaggio and Walter W. Powell, "The Iron Cage Revisited: Institutional Isomorphism and Collective Rationality in Organizational Fields," *American Sociological Review* 48 (1983), 147–60.

11. Douglas Alan Walrath, *Leading Churches Through Change* (Nashville: Abingdon Press, 1979), chap. V.

12. William Strauss and Neil Howe, *Generations: The History of America's Future, 1584–2069* (New York: Quill/William Morrow, 1991).

13. Leonard Greenhalgh, "Organizational Decline," in Samuel B. Bacharach, ed., *Research in the Sociology of Organizations: A Research Annual,* volume 2 (Greenwich, Conn.: JAI Press, 1982), 232.

14. Terrence E. Deal and Allen A. Kennedy, *Corporate Cultures: The Rites and Rituals of Corporate Life* (Reading, Mass.: Addison-Wesley, 1982).

15. McCann, *Church and Organization,* 136.

16. Adizes, *Corporate Lifecycles,* 115–33.

17. Edgar Schein, *Organizational Culture and Leadership* (San Francisco: Jossey-Bass, 1992), chap. 2.

18. Thomas Kuhn, *The Structure of Scientific Revolutions,* 2d ed., enlarged (Chicago: University of Chicago Press, 1970), chap. 1.

19. Walrath, *Leading Churches through Change,* chap. 2.

CHAPTER 7

1. Charles M. Olsen, *Transforming Church Boards into Communities of Spiritual Leaders,* (n.p.: Alban Institute, 1995).

2. William R. Myers, *Black and White Styles of Youth Ministry: Two Congregations in America,* foreword by Thomas Kochman, introduction by Charles R. Foster (New York: Pilgrim Press, 1991).

3. Ibid., 170–71.

4. Ibid., 147.

5. Ibid., 117–18.

6. Social-scientific biblical criticism has been extensive over the last generation. See, for instance, Richard L. Rohrbaugh, *The Biblical Interpreter: An Agrarian Bible in an Industrial Age* (Philadelphia: Fortress Press, 1978); Bruce Malina, *The New Testament World: Insights from Cultural Anthropology, 3d ed.* (Louisville: Westminster John Knox Press, 2001); and Carl S. Dudley and Earl Hilgert, *New Testament Tensions and the Contemporary Church* (Philadelphia: Fortress Press, 1987).

7. John M. Buchanan, *Being Church, Becoming Community* (Louisville: Westminster John Knox Press, 1996).

8. Ibid., 62–65.

9. Ibid., 64.

Other Books from THE PILGRIM PRESS

HOW TO GET ALONG WITH YOUR CHURCH
Creating Cultural Capital for Doing Ministry

GEORGE B. THOMPSON JR.

ISBN 0-8298-1437-X/paper/176 pages/$17.00

This resource incorporates Thompson's research and observations on pastoring a church. He finds that the pastors who are most successful in engaging their parishioners are the ones who develop "cultural capital" within their congregations, meaning that they invest themselves deeply into how their church conducts its life and ministries.

FUTURING YOUR CHURCH
Finding Your Vision and Making It Work

GEORGE B. THOMPSON JR.

ISBN 0-8298-1331-4/paper/128 pages/$14.95

This resource allows church leaders to explore their congregation's heritage, its current context, and its theological bearings. Dr. Thompson provides insights that enable church members to discern what God is currently calling the church to do in this time and place. It is a practical, helpful tool for futuring ministry.

THE GENERATION DRIVEN CHURCH
Evangelizing Boomers, Busters, and Millennials

WILLIAM AND LE ETTA BENKE

ISBN 0-8298-1509-0/paper/128 pages/$13.00

The Benkes seek to revitalize the ministries of small and mid-size churches by helping them to adjust to the changing culture. The book also offers strategic approaches that will re-orient ministries to attract younger generations and take churches with an "inward focus," (churches devoid of conversion growth because of the absence of meaningful outreach to un-churched adults who comprise the post-modernist cultures) to an "outreach focus."

BEHOLD I DO A NEW THING
Transforming Communities of Faith

C. KIRK HADAWAY

ISBN 0-8298-1430-2/paper/160 pages/$15.00

Recent talk and thinking about congregations concentrate on declining church attendance. Author Kirk Hadaway thinks an important part of the conversation is missing—how can churches, in spite of the decline, remain engaged in the mission of transforming lives? Looking at churches in new ways and holding new expectations will allow churches leadership to guide congregations in the journey where transformation and renewal is constant and embraced.

THE BIG SMALL CHURCH BOOK
DAVID R. RAY

ISBN 0-8298-0936-8/paper/256 pages/$15.95

Over sixty percent of churches have fewer than seventy-five people in attendance each Sunday. *The Big Small Church Book* contains information on everything from practical business matters to spiritual development. Clergy and lay leaders of big churches can learn much here as well.

LEGAL GUIDE FOR DAY-TO-DAY CHURCH MATTERS
A Hand Book for Pastors and Church Leaders – Revised and Expanded

CYNTHIA S. MAZUR AND RONALD K. BULLIS

ISBN 0-8298-1550-4/paper/148 pages/$10.00

This book belongs on every pastor's desk because the church is not exempt from the growing number of lawsuits filed each year. The authors are clergy as well as attorneys.

To order these or any other books from The Pilgrim Press, call or write to:

The Pilgrim Press
700 Prospect Avenue East
Cleveland, Ohio 44115-1100

PHONE ORDERS: 1-800-537-3394 (M–F, 8:30 AM–4:30 PM ET)

FAX ORDERS: 216-736-2206

Please include shipping charges of $4.00 for the first book and $0.75 for each additional book.

Or order from our Web site at <www.pilgrimpress.com> and <www.ucpress.com>

Prices subject to change without notice.

Organizing for Social Change — 2nd
    Bolo et al

1 — Tiannamen Sq
        typic